NO MORE ANGER!

NO MORE ANGER!

Be Your Own Anger Management Coach

Gladeana McMahon

Cognitive Behavioural Therapy

KARNAC

First published in 2008 by
Karnac Books Ltd
118 Finchley Road, London NW3 5HT

British Library Cataloguing in Publication Data

A C.I.P. for this book is available from the British Library

ISBN: 978 1 88575 430 0

Edited, designed, and produced by The Studio Publishing Services Ltd, www.publishingservicesuk.co.uk
e-mail: studio@publishingservicesuk.co.uk

Printed in Great Britain

10 9 8 7 6 5 4 3 2 1

www.karnacbooks.com

Contents

Contents

—

To all the clients who have allowed me to help them, and to Mike, without whose support I would never have managed to achieve all that I have

About the author

The *Independent on Sunday* and *Sunday Observer* listed 'life doctor' Gladeana McMahon as one of the UK's top ten coaches. She combines academic rigour with down-to-earth communication skills, and has provided therapy and coaching to politicians, celebrities, senior business people, and those in the media.

A Fellow and Vice President of the Association for Coaching, she holds Fellowships with the British Association for Counselling and Psychotherapy (BACP), the Royal Society of Arts (RSA), and the Institute of Management Studies (IMS). She is a BACP Senior Registered Practitioner, Accredited Counsellor and Supervisor, and a BABCP Accredited Cognitive–Behavioural Psychotherapist who is UKCP and UKRC registered. She is also a Certified NLP Coach and NLP Master Practitioner.

Gladeana is Head of Coaching for Fairplace, Co-Director of the Centre for Stress Management and Centre for Coaching, and is an Honorary Visiting Lecturer in the Psychology Department of the University of East London, where she taught on the Diploma and Masters' programmes for many years.

An internationally published author, she has written, edited, or contributed to over twenty books on a range of subjects. Her media work includes having presented shows such as *Ease the Load*, *Dial a Mum*, and *Sex and Soaps*. She has also been the Confidence Coach for BBC1's *Get Smarter in a Week*, and Counsellor for their 20-part series *Life's Too Short*. She is currently the Anger Management Coach for Channel 5's *Trisha Goddard Show*, and Life Coach and Stress Coach for the GMTV and Channel Four websites.

INTRODUCTION

What's special about a cognitive–behavioural approach?

The problem with using words like counselling or psychotherapy is that these words suggest there is only one method of therapy. However, at the last count there were some 450 different therapeutic approaches, some sharing ideas in common and others being as different as chalk and cheese.

Cognitive–Behaviour Therapy is a relatively new therapy. Behaviour Therapy came first in the mid-1950s, aimed originally at helping people deal with the symptoms of depression by changing the things that they did. Although Behaviour Therapy was a movement forward as it provided many people with real benefits, it also became apparent that something was lacking, and this turned out to be the attention to the person's individual thoughts that accompanied his or her behaviour.

In the late 1960s, Cognitive Therapy came into being and this therapy focused on the types of thinking styles that caused people distress. It was not long before the benefits of Behaviour and Cognitive Therapy came together, forming what is now called Cognitive–Behaviour Therapy – often referred to as CBT. Cognitive Behaviour Therapy is the only therapy that has sought assessment and validation through research, its practitioners believing it important that a therapy should not only work but should demonstrate how it works and why. As with all therapies, it has developed from its origins as a way of helping people with depression to a therapy that can help individuals with a number of mental health conditions. There are now many studies supporting the view that the best treatment for a range of conditions is CBT, and, indeed, the National Institute for Health and Clinical Excellence (NICE) and the National Health Service (NHS) have both recommended CBT as the treatment of choice when working with conditions such as depression, anxiety, and anger.

In one study undertaken by Richard Beck and Ephrem Fernandez on the effectiveness of CBT in relation to anger, it was found that the average CBT recipient was better off than 76% of untreated subjects in terms of anger reduction. In a number of additional studies, CBT was shown to have a marked effect in reducing anger and its consequent problems.

In 2002, Professors Windy Dryden and Stephen Palmer, together with Michael Neenan (Co-director of the coaching programme at the Centre for Coaching) and myself, went on to consider ways in which Cognitive Behaviour Therapy could be adapted into a coaching approach that we named Cognitive Behavioural Coaching (CBC). By adapting many of the strategies associated with CBT, we were able to put together a model that helped individuals get the best from everyday life. In addition, by integrating aspects from the new field of Positive Psychology, which aims to increase an individual's basic appreciation of life and general happiness, we were able to produce a model that worked for everyone and not just those with an identifiable mental health problem.

HOW WILL THIS BOOK HELP ME?

This book takes the skills and techniques of Cognitive Behavioural Therapy and Cognitive Behavioural Coaching and offers you the opportunity of taking control of your anger. The book aims to help you understand what is happening to you and teach you how you can overcome your anger. If you use the skills outlined in this book you will learn how to become your own anger management coach.

Some of you may find it helpful to read the book through once before returning to do the exercises. Others may find it more helpful to tackle each of the exercises as they come up. It is up to you to decide which method suits you best. What is important is that you work through the book at your own pace and in your own way, making sure that whatever way you choose ensures that you understand each and every chapter and exercise. Change will only come about if you practise the skills in your everyday life. Don't expect your behaviour to change overnight, because it took you time to be the person you are and it will take time to change yourself. Be realistic and praise yourself for every change, however small you think it is. Remember that you are doing something positive to coach yourself, and even if you think you may never manage to change, you have taken the first step in doing so.

For some people, using the skills in this book may be enough to become anger-free. For others, the book will help to reduce the anger you experience. For some readers, this book may make little difference at all. If you are in this last group, do not see this as a failure on your part, but rather as an indication that you require specialist help and need to see a Cognitive–Behavioural Therapist. The fact that you are reading this book means that you want to do something about your difficulties surrounding your anger, and if you have that kind of motivation then specialist anger management counselling is likely to be of great benefit to you.

What materials will I need?

You will find it helpful to get yourself a journal or an A4 loose-leaf folder that you can use to write down your thoughts and track your progress. As I have said, change does not happen overnight and there will be times when you may feel that you are not making as much progress as you thought. However, by keeping all your work in one place you will be able to see that, even if you are having a bad day or two, changes are happening, just maybe not as quickly as you would want. Remember that bad days get shorter and good days get longer, but there are likely to be setbacks as this is normal. Your journal or folder is a good way of capturing the total picture, and using this will help you maintain a realistic appraisal of what you have managed to achieve. In addition, research has shown that if people write things down, they are more likely to achieve the goals they set for themselves.

WHAT IS ANGER?

Too much of a good thing – the stress response

Anger can be a good thing. For example, if I go to cross the road and see a car speeding towards me, I would experience all the physical and emotional sensations of stress, and, for some, these feelings would immediately translate into feeling angry at the person driving the car. However, if I felt the same way while waiting in a queue, or find myself screaming and shouting inappropriately at the bus conductor because the bus is late, then these would not be helpful or appropriate responses. Anger is a crucial survival mechanism and our bodies are pre-programmed to protect us from dangerous situations.

Biologically, our bodies produce several stress hormones, for example, adrenaline, that encourage changes in our physical and mental state, helping us either to escape from the situation or to face it head-on. This is called the 'stress response', and you may have heard it called 'fight or flight'. The three key players when it comes to stress hormones are adrenaline (associated with flight), noradrenaline (associated with fight), and cortisol.

When this type of reaction occurs, we often feel muscle tension and experience increased heart rate, breathing, and blood pressure. We may sweat and experience changes in our digestive system, such as the feeling of 'butterflies' in the stomach. Our thinking may become more focused on the task ahead and we may be able to do things that we would not normally be able to. You may have heard stories of people who have undertaken superhuman feats to save a loved one. For example, a colleague is trapped in a fire under a cabinet that has fallen on him and a friend is able to lift the cabinet to free him – yet under normal circumstances it would be far too heavy for one person to lift.

There is a third response that can be triggered, called the 'freeze' response, where the person stops and becomes very still. Although this is a less common response, it can be very effective in the right circumstances – for example, if you were hiding from an attacker.

Like anything in life, too much of a good thing can become a problem. The stress response is essential, and yet for many it has become a burden rather than a blessing.

Figure 1 shows you what happens to your body when it experiences the stress response.

The stress response is meant only for short-term use, so if it is not switched off when the danger passes a number of problems can occur and our ability to cope lessens (see Figure 2).

The physical, mental, and behavioural sensations associated with 'fight or flight' that are essential for managing crisis situations turn into something quite different when the stress response is not turned off (see Table 1 for a list of symptoms).

So, what exactly happens to my body when I become angry?

Anger is experienced in our bodies as well as in our minds and there is a complex series of physiological changes that occurs as we become angry.

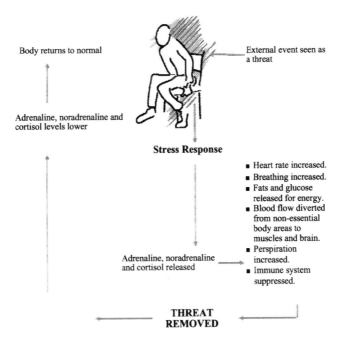

Body returns to normal

External event seen as a threat

Adrenaline, noradrenaline and cortisol levels lower

Stress Response

- Heart rate increased.
- Breathing increased.
- Fats and glucose released for energy.
- Blood flow diverted from non-essential body areas to muscles and brain.
- Perspiration increased.
- Immune system suppressed.

Adrenaline, noradrenaline and cortisol released

THREAT REMOVED

Figure 1.   The stress response.

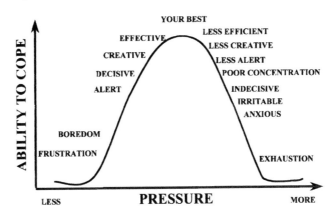

YOUR BEST

EFFECTIVE

LESS EFFICIENT

CREATIVE

LESS CREATIVE

LESS ALERT

DECISIVE

POOR CONCENTRATION

ALERT

INDECISIVE

IRRITABLE

ANXIOUS

BOREDOM

FRUSTRATION

EXHAUSTION

ABILITY TO COPE

PRESSURE

LESS

MORE

Figure 2.   Personal performance levels

Table 1. Symptoms of stress

Physical signs	Emotional signs
Tightness in chest	Mood swings
Chest pain and/or palpitations	Feeling anxious/worrying more
Indigestion	Feeling tense
Breathlessness	Feeling angry
Nausea	Feeling guilty
Muscle twitches	Feelings of shame
Aches and pains	Having no enthusiasm
Headaches	Becoming more cynical
Skin conditions	Feeling out of control
Recurrence of previous illnesses/allergies	Feeling helpless
Constipation/diarrhoea	Decrease in confidence/ self-esteem
Weight loss or weight gain	Poor concentration
Change in menstrual cycle for women	
Fainting	
Tiredness	

Behaviour	Thoughts/psychological aspects
Drop in work performance	"I am a failure'
More inclined to become accident-prone	'I should be able to cope'
Drinking and smoking more	'Why is everyone getting at me?'
Overeating/loss of appetite	'No one understands'
Change in sleeping patterns	'I don't know what to do'
Poor time management	'I can't cope'
Too busy to relax	Loss of judgement
Stuttering	Withdrawing from family and friends
Loss of interest in sex	Poor judgement
Inability to express feelings	A sense of being on a kind of 'automatic pilot'
Emotional outbursts and over-reactions	
Nervous habits such as drumming fingers	

All our emotions begin inside two almond-shaped structures in our brains that are called the amygdala. The amygdala is the part of the brain responsible for identifying threats to our well-being, and for sending out an alarm when threats are identified so that we can take steps to protect ourselves. The amygdala is so good at sending out warning signals about possible threats that we often react before the part of the brain responsible for thought and judgement (the cortex) is able to check on whether our actions are reasonable or not. This could be seen as a case of 'act first and think later', which means that we do not have time to consider the consequences of our behaviour.

Just because our bodies react in this manner, it should not be seen as an excuse for our unhelpful behaviour, since, if that were the case, people could do whatever they wanted when they wanted. However, people can and do control their aggressive impulses, and you can too. Managing anger properly is a skill that has to be learned.

As you become angry, your body's muscles tense up. Inside your brain, neurotransmitter chemicals known as catecholamines get released so that you experience a spurt of energy lasting up to several minutes. This energy is behind the desire to take immediate protective action. Your heart rate accelerates, your blood pressure rises, and your rate of breathing increases. Your face can become flushed as increased blood flow prepares you for physical action. Your attention becomes focused on what you perceive to be the target of your anger. Additional brain neurotransmitters and hormones (such as adrenaline and noradrenaline) are released, triggering a state of arousal, and you are now ready to fight.

9

Gladeana McMahon

Some statistics about anger

According to an article in the *Sunday Times Magazine* in July 2006, 45% of us regularly lose our temper at work, 64% of Britons working in an office have experienced office rage, 27% of nurses have been attacked at work, 33% of Britons are not on speaking terms with their neighbours, one in twenty of us has had a fight with the person living next door, and UK airlines reported 1,486 significant or serious acts of air rage in a year, a 59% increase over the previous year. The UK has the second-worst road rage in the world, after South Africa. More than 80% of drivers say they have been involved in road rage incidents; 25% have committed an act of road rage themselves. Seventy-one per cent of internet users admit to having suffered net rage. Fifty per cent of us have reacted to computer problems by hitting our PC, hurling parts of it around, screaming, or abusing our colleagues.

So, just how angry am I?

Although you are already aware that you have some difficulty with anger (otherwise you would not be reading this book), Table 2 provides you with a check-list of signs that outline just how much difficulty you really have. The more ticks you have, the more difficulty you are likely to experience.

Place a tick against any of the following statements that you believe apply to you.

Table 2. Signs that you have difficulties with your anger

Signs	Tick boxes
Actions	
I shout at people	☐
I argue a lot	☐
I have hit people	☐
I have had to leave a situation for fear of doing something I will regret	☐
I have slammed doors and hit objects	☐
I have said something I regret later	☐
I have hurt myself in some way	☐
I have bottled my feelings up	☐
I have said hurtful things	☐
Thoughts	
I/you have spoiled everything	☐
He/she has made me look foolish	☐
He/she deserved what I did/said	☐
You can never trust people	☐
It's not fair	☐
Feelings	
Irritability	☐
Anger	☐
Rage	☐
Feeling tense and uptight	☐
Psychological factors	
Loss of concentration	☐
Life seems like one big problem	☐
Muddled thinking as a result of anger	☐
Bodily sensations	
Tight chest	☐
Pounding heart	☐
Churned up stomach	☐
Tense muscles	☐
Feeling hot	☐
Legs feel weak	☐

Are some people more susceptible?

There is still much research required to assess whether some people are genetically predisposed to anger. There is some evidence to suggest that this may be the case, since, for example, research demonstrates that mothers who experience extreme stress while pregnant pass on an excess of stress hormones to their unborn child, which, in turn, makes the child less tolerant to withstanding stress. People who are stressed often experience increased irritability and outbursts of anger, so, in this sense, you could say that some individuals do have a predisposition towards anger, or, rather, that they have less natural protection against it. It is also common for parents to comment about how each child in their family is so different in temperament to the others, and how some children never seemed to cry and slept through the night while others screamed all the time and never seemed to sleep. Therefore, it does seem reasonable to make the assumption that there may well be additional genetic components connected with anger that have not yet come to light.

However, there are a number of factors associated with the unhelpful experience and expression of anger. These are family history, stressful life events, thinking style, poor coping skills, individual personality, and lack of social support. Even if the geneticists go on to discover other biological factors that predispose an individual towards anger, it is important to understand that a predisposition does not have to be a life sentence. For example, an individual could be predisposed towards a condition like diabetes, but if that person eats well, exercises, and leads a healthy lifestyle, they may never go on to get the disease.

Therefore, it is important to recognize that, even if some people are more predisposed towards an irritable or angry way of being, this does not necessarily mean they automatically have to be a victim of their predisposition.

Family history

Research tends to show that anger often runs in families. As yet, no one really knows how much this is due to genetic influences and how much to learning angry behaviours and thinking style from family members. Even if you are born into a family that is predisposed to feeling and expressing anger, it does not automatically mean that you are doomed for life to become an angry person. Much of our behaviour is learnt, and, if a behaviour or way of thinking can be learnt, it can be unlearnt and new behaviours developed if the individual is prepared to put in some work.

Stressful life events

Everyone experiences stressful periods from time to time. Sometimes these events take the form of bereavement, job loss, or relationship problems. Any event where we feel threatened is likely to spark off feelings of anger as well as anxiety. Psychologists discovered that even pleasant experiences, such as having a child or gaining a promotion, could be stressful because they also contain change; too much change, even positive change, requires a degree of emotional readjustment.

Thinking style

People who think in certain ways are more likely to feel angry. Such thinking styles include the ability to discount the positive (always putting down or dismissing anything positive that is said) or maximizing negative events by being overly pessimistic and dramatic. In particular, beliefs about justice and fairness, and whether we see people as basically benevolent or out to get us, are likely to trigger angry feelings. (There will be more about this type of negative thinking and the relevant antidotes later in this book.) Research has shown that there is a strong link between what you think and the mood you feel. The more negative the thinking, the more anger a person is likely to feel, particularly when the thoughts are based on perceptions of threat or on injustice. For example, John a thirty-eight-year-old financial controller, was made redundant when his department was outsourced to another country. He made a large number of applications to other firms and got a number of interviews, but his redundancy money was running out and he had still not got a job. When he returned home one day, he found a letter stating that he had been unsuccessful for a post he particularly wanted and was more than qualified for, and that evening a water leak caused severe damage to his flat. At this point, all his fears about the future were triggered and, whereas some people would experience anxiety as their primary emotion, he experienced a deep sense of rage at what he saw as the injustice of his situation. If an individual's thinking style is adaptive and healthy, he or she may feel worried or frustrated, but if it is pessimistic, then, as in the case of John, anger is a more likely outcome.

Poor coping skills

Many of us have some excellent coping skills that we can call on when we need them. For example, you may have learnt that dealing with things that need to be done rather than just thinking about them decreases your feelings of anger, as it gives you a sense of control over the situation. However, most of us have some coping strategies that are unhelpful, such as drinking, smoking, or eating too much as a way of comforting ourselves.

Individual personality

Your basic personality type is likely either to help or hinder you when it comes to dealing with stress and anger. In the late 1960s, cardiologists discovered what have come to be known as Type A and Type B personalities, and, more recently, a third has been added, called the Hardy Personality. Type As are ambitious, competitive, hard driving, and more likely to ignore stress symptoms. Although Type As have a tremendous capacity when it comes to energy and drive and are often seen as highly productive by those around them, they tend to go down rather spectacularly when they become overloaded. Type Bs are more laid back and find it easier to keep matters in perspective, whereas the Hardy Personality seems to have all the attributes of a Type A, but without the susceptibility to stress.

One of the classic symptoms of a stressed Type A is irritability and anger, and even the most charismatic and normally stable Type A character can be prone to angry outbursts over the smallest of issues when they are stressed. Having said that, this does not mean that the Type B or Hardy Personality characters don't get irritable and angry – they do. However, they are less likely to be so and more likely to take action earlier to deal with whatever is getting on top of them.

Social support

Over the years, research has demonstrated that people with good support systems in the form of family and friends are far more likely to ward off the effects of crisis or trauma. The more people we have to talk to, the more we are protected from the full effect of dealing with stress on our own. A lack of a social network really shows itself in times of crisis. Very often, simply letting off a little steam to a friend or loved one early on can prevent the build up of pent-up emotion that can later express itself as extreme anger or rage.

Could I have learnt to be angry?

It is certainly possible that you could have learnt to be angry. If one of your parents tended towards irritation and anger, and seemed to get cross over the smallest of incidents, you would learn that anger is the natural response to disappointment or a strategy for getting what you want. After all, when we are children, our parents are the people we look up to and learn from. In certain situations you would have learnt that showing your anger is the way to be. In addition, you may have seen that being angry can, in certain circumstances, get you what you want and that this is the way to go about forcing people to do the things you think they should.

It might be helpful to think of childhood as a type of training course, where those who look after us are the trainers. If the trainers are well trained and able to pass on the life skills needed, we will go on to develop these skills. However, if through no fault of the trainers they do not have the skills, or are going through a bad time that stops them from being able to pass on the skills, then it is likely that we will not develop the skills we need.

Is all anger bad?

Anger can be an appropriate response – it gets things done. For example, how many laws have come into being or been changed because individuals have felt a sense of injustice or unfairness and have taken it upon themselves, either individually or by getting others involved, to bring about such change. In this sense, anger is an appropriate emotion and one that individuals and society in general can benefit from. Anger is a human emotion and, as such, is neither good nor bad; it simply is. In writing this book, my aim is to help individuals who experience excessive amounts of unhelpful anger, and who show their anger in ways that are not helpful to either themselves or others, to understand that there are better ways to deal with life.

Let me share a personal example with you. In her later years, my mother suffered from dementia, and I had taken a number of steps to ensure that she was well looked after. She had various medical support team members who visited her on a daily basis as, apart from dementia, she also had a heart condition. In addition to the medical support team, I had also arranged for people from a range of organizations to pop in to keep an eye on her, I would make regular visits over the week to ensure that all was well, and would bring her to stay with my partner and myself for one or two days at a time.

Her dementia was getting worse, and just before I went on holiday, my partner and I decided that we would bring my mother to live closer to us so that we could look after her more easily, as we lived at opposite sides of London. I had taken my mother to a day-centre, which she had liked, and which she would begin to attend once we got back from holiday. Knowing how important it is for carers to take regular breaks, we left the country satisfied that she would be safely looked after for the two weeks we were away.

The day we returned, I rang my mother, but she did not answer the phone and, after a few more phone calls, we became worried and drove over to see her. When we arrived we could not get in, and knew something was seriously wrong. Sadly, my mother had died peacefully in her sleep two days before our return. However, the support systems that I thought were in place had fallen apart. No one had been to see her for about a week, as the keys to her flat had gone missing and no one had contacted me to let me know this. Therefore, I was under the impression that my mother was well taken care of. Understandably, the funeral and associated aspects following a family member's death took priority for the first two weeks. However, once these were taken care of, I began to investigate what had happened and a whole catalogue of mistakes came to light. As they did, I found myself becoming angry that the professionals concerned had made such fundamental errors and had, in my view, neglected my mother. Knowing that anger can be used for good as well as destructively, I wanted something good to come from my mother's death. After all, even if the errors had not taken place, my mother would still have died, as her heart gave out in her sleep. However, I did not want another family to go through what I had experienced – having to call the police and get the door broken down to find my mother dead in bed, having been there for two days alone.

Using my anger productively, I managed to elicit a letter from the head of the service apologizing for the errors that had been made and outlining the ways in which the service would ensure they did not happen to anyone else in the future. I was not interested in the fact that I could have sued the service concerned, as money would not bring my mother back. All I wanted to know was that something good could come out of this situation, and my anger helped me ensure this happened.

When anger is used well it can be an energizing force. Can you remember the last time you felt angry? Can you recall how much energy you felt? Some people are able to tap into this energy in a useful way, using it to focus their thoughts and actions in ways that have a positive outcome and do not hurt, upset, or embarrass them or anyone else. Others overdo their response, and can cause considerable distress in doing so. For example, partners may leave because they find dealing with an angry person too difficult, work relations may suffer as colleagues find it hard to deal with angry outbursts, we may feel guilty because we know that even though we do not harm our children physically, we scare them with our emotional outbursts. There are many ways in which anger can damage our relationships with others and our success in life.

In addition, many individuals, following an angry outburst, feel bad about the way that they have behaved. I have often heard clients say things like '*I felt embarrassed once I had calmed down*'; '*I behaved badly and I hate myself for doing so*'; '*I could not believe I behaved the way I did and what must people think of me*'; '*They must have thought I was mad*'; '*What am I doing to my child – she looked really scared*'.

Anger can mask anxiety

Anger can often mask feelings of anxiety and, although this point has been made earlier in the book, I believe it warrants a section all to itself to bring the point home. As mentioned above, when we perceive a threat we respond in one of two ways – flight or fight. However, both mechanisms are based on our sense of fear that something threatening or dangerous is about to happen. Sometimes the best way of dealing with a situation is to stay and confront it, using the anger we feel to deal with the perceived threat. Sometimes the best thing we can do is to run away, and when we do this it is our anxiety that tells us to retreat. Both responses are appropriate in the right circumstances. However, *both* are based on fear and perceived threat.

Angry people just show their fear in a different way to the one that most people would expect. After all, when you think about being scared, you probably think about someone running away, looking scared, feeling anxious, and generally giving off all the signs of fear. However, you can experience the same emotions and yet find yourself acting aggressively. When we do this, the appearance to the outside world is one of aggression, and most people would not think of aggression as a manifestation of anxiety. However, it often is, and so angry people get misunderstood very easily. After all, it is easier to be kind to someone who looks scared than it is to someone who seems aggressive. When people seem aggressive, we either want to get away from that person or stand up to them, which can escalate the situation, making the angry person feel even more scared or misunderstood, which can, in turn, increase his or her angry response.

Is it possible to change from being passive to being angry?

What sometimes confuses people is that it is possible to change from being a basically calm person, or even someone who has been very passive in his or her dealings with others, to someone who gets increasingly angry. Sometimes this change comes about as a reaction to severe stress or in response to a traumatic incident. However, sometimes it comes about through what could be called the 'pendulum swing'. Old-fashioned grandfather clocks have a pendulum that swings backwards and forwards, and sometimes when a person begins a change process, such as changing from being a passive person to a more active one – say perhaps through attending an assertiveness class or simply due to a change in mental attitude, the individual sometimes finds him or herself moving over a period of time from passivity to anger before finding the balance in the middle of becoming assertive.

Such changes are not a reason to avoid learning how to become assertive, as assertiveness will, in the long term, pay dividends. Sometimes this type of swing happens because an individual has felt put down and powerless for so long that, when he or she discovers that it is possible to gain control, it is akin to being given a powerful motorbike, which is exciting but also difficult to get to grips with. On the one hand, the person may enjoy the sense of exhilaration, but, on the other, may find that learning to keep the bike upright takes time! It can be hard for other people to appreciate the liberation and fear that can come with suddenly discovering that you no longer need to be a doormat.

WAYS THAT ANGER CAN
SHOW ITSELF

Irritability

Irritability, although associated with anger, is not at all like anger. For example, I may feel irritated because someone pushes in front of me in a queue, or because the gas man has not arrived at the specified time, or because it is the third time today I have had to tidy up after the children. When we are irritable we feel unsettled, and may grumble a little about what has happened. I may say something to the person who pushed in, or ring the gas service to complain, or tell my children that they need to learn to be more thoughtful. However, our comments are more measured than they would be if we were angry, rather than merely irritated. If we have a headache, we may find ourselves with less patience than we would normally have, so that things that would normally not bother us or that we would normally take in our stride seem more annoying than normal. When we are irritable, it is usually only passing and associated with an event or a general 'under the weather' feeling. Irritability does not have a great effect on the individual's well-being or that of others.

Words commonly associated with irritability are: ill humour, impatience, prickliness, touchiness.

Frustration

Frustration is more likely to happen when we are feeling as if we are being obstructed in some way. Perhaps we have waited for a handyman to complete certain tasks and had been looking forward to these being completed before Christmas as we had plans about how to make the house look nice, and then he or she keeps on putting off coming so that we are disappointed. Here we feel as if something outside of our control is frustrating our attempts to achieve the things we want. Perhaps we have all the skills to undertake a course of training, but then find out that because one of our grades is not good enough the rules say we have to undertake some additional training. For example, there are many talented and well-trained asylum seekers who have to take conversion courses because there is no yardstick in this country for their knowledge of their chosen profession to be checked. If there were, then they would be eligible for work immediately, but because there are not, they may have to undertake another long training programme simply to fulfil the stated requirements of employers here. In such circumstances it is understandable that a person would feel frustrated, as the system or process seems at fault.

Again, frustration does not have any significant impact on the well-being of the individual or others. Frustration could, however, be the first step to becoming angry if the feelings persist and escalate, although this is unlikely.

Words associated with frustration are: disappointed, discouraged, discontented, resentful.

Anger

Anger is very specific, as it relates to a strong physical, emotional, and psychological reaction. Here, the individual is unlikely to be able to contain what he or she feels, and is likely to make such feelings known by engaging inappropriate behaviour. In addition, the individual experiences strong physical sensations that, although invigorating in the short term, are tiring in the longer term. Anger could be short-lived, or could linger, depending on the circumstances and the personality of the individual concerned. When people are angry it is still possible to remain on the right side of a situation, as, although other people are likely to recognize that the person is angry, the individual may well be able to contain his or her emotion by not acting aggressively.

Words commonly associated with anger are: outrage, ill temper, incense, rile.

Rage

When someone experiences rage it means that his or anger has got out of control, and this is when it is likely that violence could be associated with such a feeling. Road rage is a good example of this – here, an individual forgets about his or her own safety and the safety of others and is simply intent on making a point. Forget about social rules and niceties, or the fact that such behaviour is against the law and could lead to imprisonment, all the individual is concerned about is evening up what he or she sees as the score. By the time a state of rage has been reached, the person who has lost control is experiencing the full range of emotional, psychological, and physical sensation. 'Red mist' is the term that has been associated with rage, as many people have commented on the feeling of being taken over by feelings of rage that it is as if a mist descends which makes it difficult for them to see what is in front of them. When people are in this state, no amount of reason will stop them from acting, and this is when an individual is at his or her most dangerous and is likely to act aggressively.

Words associated with rage are: frenzy, fury, uncontrollable, madness.

Psychological conditions that have anger associated with them

Post traumatic stress disorder (PTSD)

Post traumatic stress is often experienced following a traumatic incident. A traumatic incident is one where the person was involved in, or witnessed, an event that involved serious threat of death to a loved one or self. PTSD often happens when a person feels intense fear, helplessness, or a sense of horror. For many people, the feelings following a traumatic event pass within the first 4–6 weeks, often without any help. However, for some, the feelings do not pass and may even get worse. For these people, the sense of fear leads them to avoid people, places, and things that remind them of the event. In addition, people may also experience 'flashbacks' of some aspect of the traumatic event. It is not unusual for people with PTSD to suffer from other anxiety conditions and also to experience irritability and anger. As stated above, anger is often based on fear, but may also be a feeling in its own right. For example, if someone has been raped or has been the victim of a foreseeable accident, a sense of rage at the person who is deemed responsible may well manifest itself.

Depression

Most people assume that when someone is depressed they are quiet and sad, but, although this is true, there are many states associated with depression. By the time someone is so low that they may not even be able to get out of bed, they will have gone through a number of emotional stages, and depressed people can often manifest signs of irritability and anger before they become fully depressed.

Burn-out

Burn-out is the term used to describe someone who is suffering from extreme stress that tends to be built up over a period of time. As you will be aware from the stress response discussed earlier, when we perceive a threat we produce stress hormones to deal with the situation. If a person finds him or herself exposed to stressful life situations for a prolonged period of time, a condition called burn-out can occur. Along with depression and anxiety, anger is one of the common emotional and psychological symptoms associated with this condition.

Physical conditions

It is possible that, with chemical and biological changes that can take place due to illness, a person may feel angry and act in an angry or irritable fashion. For example, people with undiagnosed diabetes often experience mood swings, including anger. People with hyperthyroidism, where the thyroid gland works too hard, may become agitated and irritable, and sometimes a brain tumour can change someone's behaviour and mood. Anger may also manifest itself in cases of dementia and following a head injury. All of these are physical conditions, but they also have an effect on the way a person feels and behaves. It is therefore advisable for someone whose general character appears to be changing to see a doctor, just in case the changes are physical rather than emotional or psychological in nature.

Life events

Bereavement

When someone experiences bereavement, it is not unusual for the individual to experience feelings of anger. This can be directed at the deceased person (*'Why has she left me?'*), or at those around. Family members or people involved in caring for the dying person may receive the anger of the bereaved person (*'Why did you not do more?'*).

FREQUENTLY ASKED QUESTIONS

Can my anger harm me?

There are a number of studies that have shown that angry people can harm themselves. A recent study found that being angry could, in the long term, harm lung function, and other studies have shown a link between anger and coronary heart disease. There certainly do seem to be a number of physical problems associated with being angry and that is not surprising when you consider that muscle tension and an increase in heart rate, breathing, and blood pressure are all present when a person becomes angry.

In addition, if anger turns to physical violence, then an individual is also more likely to become injured.

Will I have a nervous breakdown?

Anger does not cause problems like nervous breakdowns. Many people who suffer from mental illness may feel angry, but anger itself does not cause mental illness; it is more of a by-product of the illness. For example, if someone is experiencing bouts of anger due to suffering post traumatic stress disorder, then it is possible that the individual may need psychiatric or psychological care of some description, but his or her anger is attributable to the condition and is not something that is the cause of it.

Why do I feel so tired?

Anger is a tiring emotion to experience. Your body is working hard producing and coping with a range of stress hormones and their effects. It is hard to cope with life when you are angry. Once you are able to manage your anger, you have more energy. Although you may feel energized when you are angry, the surge of stress hormones that you produce at the time and your subsequent behaviours tire the body, and it is therefore not surprising that you may feel drained following an angry episode.

Can I really learn to control my anger?

Yes, it is possible to learn to control your anger and even to eradicate it. Once you have practised your anger management techniques, you will gain more control over your feelings, your body, and your life. Having said that, it is true that some people find it harder than others, and have to work harder to get their anger under control, and for some, anger will modify itself into feelings of irritability.

What about medication – isn't there a pill that will cure me?

The only real way to deal effectively and in the long term with your anger is to learn to live your life differently. However, if your anger is a by-product of another condition, such as depression or stress, then medication may well help, as by dealing with these conditions you will also deal with the anger that is only a symptom. Some people believe that tranquillizers will help. However, apart from the fact that doctors do not prescribe tranquillizers for long-term use because they can be addictive, the problem with taking medication is that if you do not deal with the cause and change this, then the medication does not cure anything. All it may do is provide a temporary decrease in angry feelings, which fades once the medication is stopped.

Can alcohol help calm me?

Using alcohol to try to calm down is counter-productive. Alcohol often exaggerates the feelings we have, and can also act as a de-inhibitor. How often have people told stories about something they said to another person that they thought better of when they were sober? Alcohol is a drug, and when we take it we alter our bodies and our minds. If you consider the relationship between alcohol and violence (just visit an Accident and Emergency Department on a weekend after the pubs close), you soon realize that alcohol does not calm a person but is likely to inflame existing bad feeling.

As a general rule, people who are experiencing anger-related difficulties should steer well clear of alcohol or other mood altering drugs.

BECOMING ANGER-FREE

Help yourself to manage stress

As stress is likely to make anger worse, or even be the cause of an angry outburst, it is important to learn how to deal with stress. Help yourself by remembering that you can always take *some action* to minimize, even if by only a small amount, the stress you experience. Additional tips on how to manage stress are provided in the section 'Stress busting' (pp. 158–160). The following strategies are those which are particularly useful to people who experience anger as their initial response to stress.

Come to your own aid by:

A anticipating stressful activities and planning for them;
I identifying the major sources of stress in your life;
D developing a range of coping strategies that you can use on a regular basis so you become familiar with them and can call upon them when you really need them.

Techniques and strategies for managing anger related to stress

You can choose from the following range of techniques to suit your own preferences and circumstances.

Use your support systems

Maintain or establish a strong support network. Come to terms with your feelings and share them with others. Ask for help when you need it and accept it when it is offered. You can always offer help to other people when you are stronger and they need it. For now, it's your turn to accept help.

Research has shown that people who have strong support networks are able to withstand the pressures of life more effectively than those who do not.

Relaxation

Relaxation can also play an important part in dealing with stress and in managing anger. Simple ways in which you can find time for yourself are:

- take time to enjoy a bath, light some candles, sprinkle a few drops of lavender aromatherapy oil into the water and play some gentle music while you take time for yourself;
- dim the lights in the lounge, play some gentle music, close your eyes and allow yourself time to relax;
- take some time to enjoy your garden or local park. Take time to look at all the trees and flowers.

Relaxation exercises

There are many forms of relaxation exercises, ranging from those that require physical exertion or movement to those that require nothing more than breathing or visualization techniques. Listed below are three common relaxation techniques.

BREATHING – A RESCUE REMEDY THAT CAN BE USED ANY TIME AND ANYWHERE

When you find yourself feeling stressed, or are about to deal with a difficult situation, it can be useful to have a strategy that can help you relax quickly and efficiently. The problem with many relaxation exercises is that you need to lie down or take time out, and this is impossible if you find yourself in a crowded tube train getting irritated with the person next to you, or if you are about to have a difficult meeting with your colleagues.

The following exercise provides you with a mechanism that, once you have practised it so that you can simply use it on demand, can be called upon to help you keep calm. Keep practising until you feel confident that you would be able to undertake this breathing exercise anywhere and at any time. It is simple but effective, and can take the edge off feelings of anger.

- Breathe in through your nose for a count of four.
- Breathe out through your mouth for a count of five.
- As you breathe out, consciously relax your shoulders.

As you breathe in and out, use your stomach muscles to control your breathing. For example, when breathing in, use your stomach muscles to push out, and when you breathe out, use your stomach muscles to push in. This way you will breathe more deeply and this will help you gain the maximum benefit from this kind of relaxation.

DIAPHRAGMATIC BREATHING

This type of breathing is similar to the one above. However, this type of breathing exercise is one that you can use at the end of a long day as a way of unwinding.

To breathe using your diaphragm, you need to draw air into your lungs so that it will expand your stomach and not your chest. It is best to take in long, slow breaths so

33

that you allow your body to absorb all of the oxygen you are inhaling, and it is best if you loosen belts, skirts, or anything tight that is likely to interfere with your ability to do this. It may not feel comfortable at first, simply because you are not used to this way of breathing. However, with practice you will really begin to feel the benefits of the relaxation this type of breathing exercise can offer you.

- Sit or lie comfortably and loosen your clothes.
- Put one hand on your chest and the other on your stomach.
- Inhale slowly through your nose.
- As you exhale, feel your stomach expand with your hand – if your chest expands then concentrate more on breathing with your stomach
- Slowly exhale through your mouth.
- Rest and repeat the exercise for between five and ten minutes.

MUSCLE TENSING EXERCISE

An American doctor, Edmund Jacobson, developed what has become known as progress muscle relaxation in the 1920s. He trained his patients to learn to voluntarily relax certain muscles in their bodies, and found the procedure helpful in alleviating a range of medical as well as psychological conditions. This exercise works on the premise that, since muscular tension accompanies strong emotions, then you could reduce those feelings by learning how to deal with such tension.

1. Lie on the floor and make yourself comfortable.

2. Starting with your feet, tense all your muscles and then relax them. Focus on how heavy your feet feel and the way in which they are sinking into the floor.

3. Tense all the muscles in your legs as hard as you possibly can, then relax them. Focus on how heavy your legs feel and the way in which they are sinking into the floor.

4. Move up along through the other parts of your body – hips, stomach, chest, arms, neck, and face – tensing and relaxing the muscles as you go.

Note: If you suffer from high blood pressure or heart problems, you should always consult your doctor before engaging in this particular exercise.

Visualization

1. Choose a safe place to sit or lie down.

2. Imagine you are in a garden at the time of the year you like best, enjoying looking at flowers, shrubs, trees, and so on.

3. You notice a wall along one side of the garden. In the middle of the wall is an old-fashioned wooden door with a wrought iron handle on it.

4. You make your way over to the door and open it.

5. On the other side, you find yourself in your own, very special, safe place. A place no one knows about and where no one can get you.

6. Enjoy being there.

7. When you are ready, make your way back to the door.

8. Leave and shut the door firmly behind you, knowing that your special safe place is always there, whenever you choose to return.

9. Walk around the garden and, when you are ready, open your eyes.

Note: This exercise can take between two minutes and half an hour – depending on how much time you wish to allocate to it.

Anchoring

'Anchoring' is a simple technique whereby you associate positive, calming, confident feelings to a particular object, usually, but not always, something you wear frequently. All that's required is that in moments of anger you touch the chosen object, and then focus on the feelings associated with it.

1. Choose an object, say, a ring.
2. Now, close your eyes and focus on some aspect of your life that brings a warm glow or a smile to your face. This could be a person, place, or an activity that makes you feel good about yourself.
3. Rub the ring as you reflect on that happy thought and continue doing so for five or more minutes.
4. Wait for a few minutes and then repeat the process.
5. In carrying out this simple routine, you will have anchored positive feelings to your chosen object. From now on, merely touching that object should bring on good feelings instantly.

Meditation

Although meditation is often thought of as a component of Eastern religions, aspects of it are now being used in a new area of Cognitive Behaviour Therapy called 'mindfulness'. There are a number of studies that have demonstrated that engaging in regular meditation changes brainwaves and that this has a calming effect.

Meditation describes a state of concentrated attention on some object, or thought, or awareness. It usually involves turning the attention inward to the mind itself. Some forms of meditation are also used alongside physical activities such as yoga.

Biofeedback

Biofeedback involves measuring bodily responses such as blood pressure, heart rate, and skin temperature/moisture. By providing physical information to the user, it allows an individual to gain control over the physical processes that he or she previously thought were automatic. The popularity of biofeedback has varied since it began being used in the 1960s. However, there is now resurgence in its use, particularly in the stress management field. Biofeedback is now being used in its most sophisticated form to help with a range of medical conditions such as attention deficit hyperactive disorder (ADHD).

However, the simplest method, that of using what are called 'biodots' (small black dots that can be used on the skin or attached to a business card and placed between thumb and forefinger), have also been found to be helpful, as they provide the individual with information on how his or her body is reacting (i.e., whether it is manifesting the signs of stress) and therefore help the person to decide on the appropriate form of action to rectify the situation. (See p. 169 for further details.)

Anger and dietary tips

Anger can be made worse by taking stimulants such as tea, coffee, colas, and chocolate, all of which contain caffeine.

Caffeine is a stimulant, and stimulants are best avoided when we are experiencing emotions such as anxiety and anger. Because we produce more adrenaline when we are feeling threatened, this can affect our blood sugar levels, and they may indeed drop dramatically. Therefore, in order to keep those levels balanced, it is important to eat 'little and often' during the day. It may also be helpful to avoid refined sugars and other substances which give too much of 'a high' too quickly. Slow-release foods such as carbohydrates (potatoes, pasta, rice, bread, apples, and bananas) are a much better idea, as they fuel the body in a more even, controlled way. (See 'The anger-free diet' section at the end of this book for further information on how you can support your anger management strategies through diet, and the 'Anger-Free Diet' on p. 161 for details.)

Managing your time

Learn to manage your time as effectively as possible. Time is a valuable commodity. How many times do you catch yourself saying, '*I'd really like to, but I don't have the time*', or '*There just aren't enough hours in the day*'? Too much activity leads to exhaustion; too little, and we become bored and frustrated. There are 168 hours in a week and 8,736 hours in a 365-day year and so, with a finite amount of time, it is important that we make the most of what we have. Many people who experience irritability and anger find that poor time management only adds to these feelings, and this is especially true when an individual is stressed. In such instances, when the person may have been working far too hard, it only takes one simple thing to go wrong, such as the printer running out of toner, to Ωsend that individual into a fit of rage. In addition, if an individual feels that he or she does not have enough time to enjoy life, but is always running around for others or trying to keep on top of a never ending workload, this, too, can tip the balance into an angry response. See the 'Time management' section (pp. 152–157) for further information on how to use time effectively.

Sleep

It is important for a person to get adequate sleep in order to foster psychological and physiological well-being. Sleep is essential for survival, health, and fitness, and research suggests that it is the quality of sleep that is most important. However, too little or too much may lead to poor performance. The amount of sleep required varies considerably from person to person. Most people sleep for seven hours; some may need nine, and others only five. Ironically, it is often the worry about losing sleep that produces more negative symptoms than the loss of sleep itself. Many people underestimate the amount of sleep they actually get due to the amount of time they spend worrying about not sleeping when they are awake.

The kind of sleep that is most important is what is called rapid eye movement (REM), which is linked to dreaming. All people dream, even if they wake without any memory of dreaming.

Stress is one of the main causes of sleep disturbance. Many people lie awake at night worrying about problems or thinking about the future in an anxious manner; then, having finally fallen asleep, wake feeling tired as the original worries are still there.

If you are experiencing difficulties sleeping, the following strategies might help.

- Ensure you have a routine. Have a warm milky drink, as milk contains tryptophan, which promotes sleep.
- Take a warm bath. Using relaxing bath oils may also help.
- Avoid sleeping during the day.
- Avoid drinking caffeine, as caffeine is a stimulant and may keep you awake. Too much coffee during the day could still affect you in the evening;
- Avoid a heavy meal and eating late at night.
- Ensure you get plenty of exercise during the day. It may be particularly helpful to take your exercise during the late afternoon or early evening.
- Use your relaxation exercises as outlined above.
- Ensure your sleeping environment is as pleasant as possible, not too hot or too cold. Switch off electrical appliances to avoid a 'mains hum'.
- Turn the clock away from you. Research has shown that turning the clock away from you helps if you are having problems sleeping, as clock-watching is liable to keep you awake, whereas not knowing what the time is encourages you to sleep more.

If you are not sleeping because of a traumatic event, you may also need to feel secure in your sleeping space. For example, ensure that all doors and windows have proper locks and are alarmed.

Some people find that changing the position of the bed or rearranging the layout of the bedroom can be helpful, as can removing objects such as pictures or ornaments that may seem frightening in a half-awake state. Remember, if your predisposition is towards anger, then although something might be frightening to one person, it may well trigger an irritable or angry response in you. Introducing pleasant smells may also create a pleasant atmosphere. Lavender oil is particularly popular, and recommended by complementary health practitioners such as aromatherapists to aid relaxation and sleep.

If you find yourself unable to sleep within forty-five minutes of going to bed, then get up and engage in another activity, such as reading. After 20–25 minutes, go back to bed again and try to get some sleep. Repeat the process, if you still have not fallen asleep, for as long as is necessary. It is important that your bed remains associated with sleeping.

People may experience nightmares following a traumatic incident. If this is the case it can be helpful to try the following exercises.

- Write down the dream in the third person (*Jane could not get away*), then in the first person voice (*I could not get away*), until you feel more comfortable with the dream.
- Think about what the dream might mean. Is it an actual replay, rather like a flashback of the traumatic incident, or is the dream completely different?
- Think about how you could change the story. For example, if you were trapped, perhaps you could find a way out or a sudden surge of strength to remove the item trapping you. Practise this new version of the dream in your imagination while you are awake.
- When you have practised your new version of the dream, then practise it again when you are tired and relaxed and before going to sleep.
- Tell yourself that you intend to replace the dream with the new ending the next time it happens.

You may find you have to repeat this exercise before it becomes fully effective. It would be helpful to keep a note, using the 0–8 scale of the emotional distress experienced, of each nightmare. You may find that if the nightmares do not stop, they may change in degrees of severity, and by keeping a note of this you can see how your nightmares are weakening.

ANGER-FREE THINKING

The four stages of change

Whenever you learn something new, regardless of whether it is a practical skill like using the Internet or a mental skill such as changing behaviour or negative beliefs, you go through a set sequence of learning:

- stage one, unconsciously incompetent;
- stage two, consciously incompetent;
- stage three, consciously competent;
- stage four, unconsciously competent.

This process is known as Robinson's Four Stages of Learning.

Stage one: unconsciously incompetent

'Don't know it and can't do it.'
  You feel unhappy but have no idea why.

Stage two: consciously incompetent

'I begin to notice just how often I have negative thoughts but I don't seem able to change anything.'
  During this stage you become aware of what is happening but seem unable to do anything about it. This is the awareness stage: for example, realizing the ways in which you make yourself feel angry by magnifying situations in a negative way, which increases your anger, but not being able to stop.

Stage three: consciously competent

'I have skills and can handle situations better although I still have to think about what I am doing.'

You now have a range of strategies to use, but you still have to think about what you are doing, as it does not feel natural.

Stage four: unconsciously competent

'I suddenly realized what I had done and how I handled the situation without even thinking about it.'

The more you practise your new skills the more your behaviour feels 'natural'. You are now working off your automatic pilot – doing things without thinking about them.

Change happens over time and it is persistence, practice and the belief in taking one small step at a time that wins the day.

Does optimism pay?

Optimists think more positively about life, seeing the good in situations and minimizing the bad. Pessimists think that optimists are foolish and optimists think that pessimists are depressing. Researchers believe that optimism and pessimism have a genetic factor. However, there is also evidence to suggest that it is the environment we are brought up in that shapes the way we think. We discussed earlier in the book the way that behaviours can be learnt, and this is true for optimists and pessimists.

There is research to suggest that there are advantages to being an optimist. For example, it would appear that optimists live longer, achieve more, and have happier lives.

When you suffer from anger, it can be hard to believe that you can ever become more optimistic about life. However, it is possible to relearn behaviours and ways of thinking. The following exercise will help you begin this process.

EXERCISE

Situations where you experience optimism and pessimism

1. Name two people you feel more optimistic around and state why.

   (i) _____

   (ii) _____

2. Identify two situations that you have felt more optimistic about and state why.

   (i) _____

   (ii) _____

3. Name two people you feel pessimistic around and state why.

   (i) _____

   (ii) _____

4. Identify two recent situations where you have felt pessimistic and state why.

   (i) _____

   (ii) _____

When you look at your answers, can you spot any patterns forming? For example, are you more optimistic with certain people but pessimistic with others?

Pessimism drains you. However, pessimistic thinking can be changed. Changing your thinking style is perfectly possible if you are prepared to put in some time and effort.

A third group has been identified: those who plan for the worst or devise a fall-back position if things don't work out as hoped. They never believe anything good will happen automatically. However, they do put themselves forward, even though they do not believe they will succeed. They work hard and prepare. These are called 'Defensive Pessimists'. Defensive pessimism seems to work for some people. If you have a go you are probably a defensive pessimist – if you don't, you are a pessimist.

The following exercise is aimed at helping you begin the process of increasing your optimistic outlook on life.

EXERCISE

Ways of improving optimism

1. Make a list of three good things that have happened to you at the end of each day. The things you list do not have to be major items, but simply tasks you may feel you have handled better than you thought you would.

2. When you find yourself looking at life pessimistically, replace your negative thought with a positive thought or image.

3. Make a list of positive statements and repeat these to yourself on a daily basis (e.g., '*I am able to conquer my anger*'; '*I can learn to think and behave differently*').

Are my thoughts real?

We try to make sense of the world around us; we interpret the messages we receive and use these to decide on the best ways of coping with our environment. Sometimes what we think is not really what is happening. There is often more than one way to look at a situation. The way we see the world shapes what we do. Once we realize this, we have more choices about the way we behave and can make better decisions.

Look at Figure 3. Is it a vase, or is it two faces looking at each other?

Perhaps you can only see one image. This exercise is rather like life. Often, we don't see what is right in front of our eyes and, even when it is pointed out, it can be hard to change our viewpoint. Time, patience and a little effort can work wonders.

Figure 3.   A vase – or two faces in profile?

Gladeana McMahon

How do my beliefs affect me?

Since the 1950s, psychologists have identified a number of beliefs that people apply to their everyday living. In the trauma field, the three 'life beliefs' which have been identified as being crucial to the speed at which a person can recover from a traumatic incident are:

- bad things happen to 'other people';
- life has meaning and purpose;
- I would always 'do the right thing' in an emergency.

All of these beliefs cause their own particular type of problems. For example, bad things *don't* just happen to 'other people' – they can happen to *anyone*. Someone has to be a statistic and *bad things happen to good people and good people sometimes do bad things*.

If you believe that 'life has meaning and purpose', then person-made disasters, acts of cruelty, or senseless bloodshed are more likely to be greatly disturbing. Such incidents seem meaningless and with no purpose. In such circumstances, then, an individual may feel very frightened, especially if he or she had always believed that life did have meaning and purpose. In these cases, depending on the individual concerned, a reaction of anger or anxiety or a mixture of both may be present.

For those who believe they would 'do the right thing' in an emergency, this belief can become challenged when they find themselves behaving in a different way to the way they would have predicted. When this is the case, the individual may experience a sense of anger at what is seen as their weakness, and this anger may also live alongside feelings of shame.

As mentioned earlier, some of these involuntary and uncontrollable reactions are pre-programmed by our biology. When we are in a life-threatening situation, our stress response kicks in and the body becomes like an alarm system. Either we flee to escape danger or we stay and stand our ground. Either way, it is almost impossible for anyone to predict with any accuracy how he/she will behave in a life-threatening situation.

Human beings tend to use beliefs to guide everyday transactions. For example, '*I will go to work and come home safely*' or, '*I will travel on the bus quite safely*'. We may find our thinking becomes distorted if our beliefs are challenged by life events that, in turn, can cause us to become hyper-aroused and hyperactive. Anxiety can be a common feature of such thinking.

People who experience anger often have beliefs along the lines of '*People must treat me fairly*'; '*If you don't show people that you are strong then they will take advantage*'; '*People are out to get you*'; '*I have to stand up for myself otherwise no one else will*'.

As mentioned earlier, beliefs are formed from the messages we receive as children from those around us. It is these messages that shape the way we think about ourselves.

Faulty thinking

There is a considerable amount of research that demonstrates a link between anger and the way we think. Let's look at the relationship between anger and thinking style by considering two people who might be waiting for a bus that is very late.

One might recognize that there is nothing that can be done, uses his mobile to phone the people he needs to, and puts it down to one of those things – he may feel irritated but, as he has decided there is nothing he can do, he starts listening to the music on his I-pod. The other gets increasingly angry and starts to think that this is awful and he is late and this should not happen. He becomes so wrapped up in his own thoughts and the increasing anger, muttering under his breath, shifting from foot to foot and feeling tense and upset that he does not think to use his mobile. Both men experience the same situation but the way they think about it either helps or hinders them.

Faulty thinking relates to the way in which we interpret situations and the following considers the ways in which we can change our thinking to that which is likely to be more effective in dealing with anger.

A good way of thinking about whether our thoughts, feelings, and associated behaviours are reasonable is to ask yourself if everyone in your situation would think, act, and feel in the same way. For example, if others might deal with a situation differently, then it is possible for you to do so, and it is likely that all that is different is the way the other person thinks about what has happened. If there are alternatives, and such alternatives would be better for you and for others, then it is possible for you to learn to think in a healthier way.

Healthy thinking

Simple as ABC

There is a model used in Cognitive–Behavioural Therapy called the ABC model (see Table 3), which describes how

Table 3.   ABC model

A Situation (trigger)	B Thoughts based on beliefs	C Consequences
Waiting at bus stop	**Thoughts** *This should not be* *happening.* **Beliefs** *The world should treat* *me better as I work so* *hard and do the right* *thing.*	**Feelings** Anger **Actions** Becoming tense, shifting weight from leg to leg and looking menacingly at others.

situations trigger thoughts, how thoughts trigger feelings, and how feelings lead to actions.

Triggers

It will be helpful to you if you can begin to identify the kinds of situations that trigger your irritation and anger. Once you have identified these, you can go on to consider whether the way you think about the situation is the cause of your anger and how you can go about changing the way that you think.

Use the following exercise to make a list of all the situations that you can identify where your response is to feel irritated or angry. If you find this a difficult exercise to complete, you may find it useful to prefix your situation with the words – 'I feel irritated or angry when . . .'

EXERCISE

I feel irritated or angry when . . .

1. _____

2. _____

3. _____

4. _____

5. _____

6. _____

7. _____

8. _____

9. _____

10. _____

Keeping an anger diary

Some of you may have found the above exercise quite easy and others may have found it quite hard. However, it is important to be able to identify the situations that cause you the greatest difficulty so that you can develop the appropriate counter-measures to eliminate or reduce your angry feelings and any unhelpful actions you then engage in.

An anger diary is a useful tool to keep track of what is happening, what triggers your anger, and how you react.

It is a way of identifying situations and what you did at the time, as this way you can build a picture of how you react and respond to your environment. Once you can identify the situations that you respond angrily to you are halfway to being able to do something about your behaviour.

It is best to write down the incidents in your diary as soon after they have happened as possible and to make your accounts of what happened as full as possible.

When you have completed your diary, read over what you have written and try to understand what it was about the situation in question that caused you to feel angry. Once you have done this, then consider alternative ways in which you could have behaved.

For example, let's look at the entries in Michael's diary below (see Table 4). In the first situation, Michael's neighbours were having a party and he found the music annoyed him as it was loud and interfered with him being able to watch the television.

There are various ways in which Michael could handle this situation either to minimize his irritation or to completely eradicate it.

1. Michael could look at the time and make a decision that 10.30 p.m. was not that late, that his neighbours did not normally make a noise, and that everyone is entitled to have a party now and again. He could consider the fact that it may have been a special event such as a birthday or anniversary party, and that if this was the case then it was nice to think that people were celebrating.

2. He could decide to put the volume up on his television or, as he had a television in his bedroom at the

53

back of his house, that he would watch TV there as it was much quieter.

3. He could make a decision that if the noise continued at the same level at midnight, he would go over and have a quiet word.

Many people who experience anger often make the mistake of thinking that they should keep quiet. However, if you have a concern and are bothered about something, then it is important that you say something if you need to. Bottling things up can make you feel like a victim, and this can fuel your anger. However, it is important to think about what you will say and how you will say it. (The section titled 'Assertiveness' later in this book will be of help to you with this, as it includes a range of techniques that can assist you to put your point of view across in the

Table 4. Michael's anger diary

Date	Time	Situation (trigger)	What I did
10.12.06	10.30 p.m.	Noisy party going on two doors away. I wanted to watch the television but the music and noise the people were making annoyed me.	Paced up and down the lounge and thought about how inconsiderate my neighbours were being.
12.12.06	12 noon	Children playing at the back of the estate.	Went outside and shouted at them. How dare they make such a noise.
14.12.06	1 p.m.	Colleagues going out to lunch.	Kept out of their way for the afternoon.

most helpful and appropriate manner.) Blank anger diary sheets are provided for you in the Appendices.

Once you have identified the kinds of situations that trigger your anger, what you do in these situations, and the kinds of thoughts that go through your head, you will gain not just an understanding but also have the option of devising strategies (behaviours and alternative ways of thinking about what has happened), so that you can minimize or totally eradicate your anger.

Negative thoughts

Much of our thinking is in the form of automatic thoughts. We use the term automatic as we are often not even aware we are thinking them. These thoughts simply seem to 'pop' into our heads. In a way it is rather like supermarket music – something in the background of which we are not really aware.

Negative automatic thoughts are often referred to as NATs. In many ways this is a good description for such thoughts as, rather like the insects, they are irritating. Although you do not often see them, their bite can irritate for days. These kinds of thoughts are usually distorted – that is to say they do not match the facts. They are involuntary and difficult to switch off.

As we have had many years to perfect our thinking style it can be hard to change the way we think. If you have ever tried to break a habit you will appreciate how hard it can be.

The role of judgements

When a situation occurs, you form a judgement of what has happened. Your thoughts about what has happened tell you that this was either a good thing, an 'all right' thing, or a bad thing, and it is these judgements of situations that may help or hinder you when it comes to your anger.

For example, if Michael judges that his neighbours are being insensitive, he is more likely to think badly of them than if he judges that they are having a good time, do not make a noise normally, and that everyone is entitled to make a noise now and again. One set of thoughts is likely to encourage him to feel resentful and angry while the other are more likely to encourage him to think in a more measured and less heated manner.

Judgements are made based on the way we think about situations and there has been a considerable amount of research into the types of thinking styles that are helpful and those that are not.

Types of negative thinking

There are many types of negative thoughts. You may find that you relate to some more than others.

All or nothing thinking

You see things in extreme terms such as good or bad, right or wrong, success or failure. You probably set impossible tasks and then feel bad when you do not achieve them. You may even not start tasks because you feel you cannot complete them to the desired standard.

For example:

- you planned a special night out and you were late meeting your partner and then it rained and you did

not have an umbrella, so you think to yourself
'*Everything is ruined*';

● you may be struggling with an assignment and you
don't like the tutor as you feel that he or she does not
have enough time for you. You do not get the mark
you were hoping for. You then say to yourself, '*What's
the point of continuing if my marks are going to be less
than they should be.*'

EXERCISE

If you decide that *all or nothing* thinking relates to
you, list two situations where you can identify this
type of thinking, together with the thoughts that
were going through your head at the time.

Situation   Thoughts at the time

1. _____

2. _____

Jumping to conclusions

This is rather like believing you are telepathic and can
read minds. You predict a negative outcome and then
encourage it to happen by telling yourself it will, and you
set up what could be called a 'self-fulfilling prophecy'.

For example:

● you have to make a comment about a project at work
and find yourself thinking about everything that
could go wrong and about your boss who always
seems to question your thinking. As you do this you

feel more and more angry at what you perceive as the unfairness of it all and then discover that all the things you have told yourself will happen come true!;

- you buy a present for your friend and although he thanks you, you get the feeling that he is not as pleased as you thought he would be. You think, '*He doesn't like it – well, stuff him.*' However, he has had some bad news and does not realize it has upset him as much as it has. Because you believe he is not appreciative of your efforts, the situation deteriorates between you.

EXERCISE

If you decide that *jumping to conclusions* relates to you, list two situations where you can identify this type of thinking, together with the thoughts that were going through your mind at the time.

    Situation   Thoughts at the time

1. _____

2. _____

Mental filter

A mental filter is like a sieve where you filter out everything that's good and focus only on the negative things that have happened.

For example:

- your friend tells you how much she valued your help with putting up some shelves but then says that she noticed that one was a little crooked. You find yourself obsessing about the one comment she made that you feel is negative while ignoring the rest;

- you want to learn to swim better but have never been that confident in the water and remember a time when your friends teased you about this. Although that was a long time ago, and there are many other examples of how quickly you learn, on the basis of this experience you predict that you will be useless and do not join the class.

EXERCISE

If you decide that *mental filter* relates to you, list two situations where you can identify this type of thinking, together with the thoughts that were going through your mind at the time.

Situation   Thoughts at the time

1. _____

2. _____

Discounting the positive

You make yourself feel unhappy by discounting your achievements and the positive things you have done. When we discount the positive we take the pleasure out of life.

For example:

- you have been working hard to learn a new software programme. However, you say to yourself, '*That was nothing, anyone could have done that.*';

- you have worked hard spring cleaning your flat for the weekend. Although you have managed to get on top of many of the items on your list it was impossible to clear them all. You tell yourself, *'I've achieved nothing really as there are still things to do.'*

EXERCISE

If you decide that *discounting the positive* relates to you, list two situations where you can identify this type of thinking, together with the thoughts that were going through your mind at the time.

Situation   Thoughts at the time

1. _____

2. _____

Emotional reasoning

You believe that what you feel is true. So if you feel bad you believe it's because you have done something wrong.

For example:

- you feel awkward about social events and conclude that other people look down on you;
- You make a mistake and you find yourself thinking, *'I made a mistake, I must be dumb.'*

Labelling

Do you label yourself with terms such as *'I am a failure'*; *'I am useless'*; and *'I am worthless'*? Every time anything goes

EXERCISE

If you decide that *emotional reasoning* relates to you, list two situations where you can identify this type of thinking, together with the thoughts that were going through your mind at the time.

	Situation	Thoughts at the time
1.	_____	
2.	_____	

wrong, however small, it reinforces the label you have given yourself.

For example:

- you did not do as well as you could have in a driving lesson and feel a failure. Because you did not do well, you say to yourself, '*I am a failure.*'
- you made a error in some calculations and because you made an error you say to yourself, '*I am stupid.*'

EXERCISE

If you decide that *labelling* relates to you, list two situations where you can identify this type of thinking, together with the thoughts that were going through your mind at the time.

	Situation	Thoughts at the time
1.	_____	
2.	_____	

61

Personalization and blame

You take everything personally and blame yourself even when it isn't your fault.

For example:

● you are in charge of organizing the office Christmas party and have had a number of setbacks caused by your friends' inability to decide on aspects of the trip. A few of your colleagues are a little agitated and you find yourself feeling irritated, thinking, '*I should have managed to organize things better and my colleagues think I have let them down.*'

Alternatively, you may blame other people for what goes wrong instead of thinking about your part in events. In this case, instead of thinking that you had let people down and feeling irritated at yourself, you find yourself thinking, '*How ungrateful, if they think they can do it better then let them do it, I won't let people treat me like this.*'

EXERCISE

If you decide that *personalization and blame* relates to you, list two situations where you can identify this type of thinking, together with the thoughts that were going through your mind at the time.

Situation   Thoughts at the time

1. _____

2. _____

Over-generalization

You tend to make global statements about yourself, other people, and the world.

For example:

- you are struggling with a new accounting system. You make a mistake and think, '*I'll never get this!*';
- your last relationship ended because you found out your girlfriend had not got over her previous relationship and think, '*Women are all the same, you cannot trust them.*'

EXERCISE

If you decide that *over-generalizing* relates to you, list two situations where you can identify this type of thinking, together with the thoughts that were going through your mind at the time.

	Situation	Thoughts at the time
1.	_____	_____
2.	_____	_____

Shoulds and musts

Your life is full of things you think you *should be doing* and *must do*. You use these statements as a way of trying to motivate yourself. However, the more you tell yourself these things the less likely you are to do them. In addition you also end up feeling bad about yourself. Some people use 'shoulds' and 'musts' as a way of thinking about other people in a punishing way. For example, '*He should have known*'; '*She must do what I want.*' When we use this type of thinking in relation to others, we are really saying we know what is right.

For example:

- you spend time believing, '*I should not feel like this at my age*'; '*I have to do better and how stupid of me.*';
- you are having a particularly difficult time and you start thinking, '*Just who do they think they are giving me such a hard time; when I work this hard others should appreciate it.*'

EXERCISE

If you decide that *shoulds and musts* relates to you, list two situations where you can identify this type of thinking, together with the thoughts that were going through your mind at the time.

	Situation	Thoughts at the time
1.		
2.		

Catastrophizing

When we use this type of thinking it is rather like making a mountain out of a molehill – if there is a way of making things as bad as possible, we think it. People using this type of thinking often use lots of emotional words that predict the most awful consequences.

For example:

- your boss says he wants to talk to you tomorrow and you spend the evening thinking about what he might want to say and psyching yourself up for a confrontation because you believe the discussion will be negative;
- you share a communal bin area in your flats and a new tenant did not see the sign that tells them to place all items in the large bins for collection. This person has just moved in and left some cardboard boxes by the bin and you believe that they have done this on purpose and that it is a big deal.

EXERCISE

If you decide that *catastrophizing* relates to you, list two situations where you can identify this type of thinking, together with the thoughts that were going through your mind at the time.

    Situation   Thoughts at the time

1. _____

2. _____

Anger-free thinking means learning how to challenge and change your negative thinking. Try to imagine that every time you engage in negative thinking it's like going to your building society, taking out a handful of money, and then giving it away without thought. Your emotional energy is just as valuable. It's when you face a crisis that you need to be able to call upon your reserves. After all, it's when the roof needs replacing that you are glad you have saved some money, and the same principle applies when you face an emotional crisis.

Edit your thoughts

Writing things down means you are more likely to stick to your plans. Buy yourself a notebook and use this to track your progress. If you keep all your information in one place it means you have an independent record of your success. Everyone has bad days, and progress hardly ever goes in a straight line upwards. There are usually some setbacks along the way.

Your first step is to learn *how to* challenge your thoughts. Using the list you made of your negative thinking under the 'self-defeating thinking' list, complete the 'faulty thinking form' below to help you identify the type of unhelpful thinking in which you are engaging.

Faulty thinking form

Situation	Self-defeating thinking	Feelings and actions	Healthy response	New approach
A	B	C	D	E

Completed example

Situation A	Self-defeating thinking B	Feelings and actions C	Healthy response D	New approach E
Someone pushes ahead of me in a queue	*Who do they think they are – no one should behave that way and it is up to me to stand up for my rights!* **Empirical:** *Where is my evidence that he meant to do this – I made an innocent mistake once, the queue is not a neat line and he came in on the other side.* **Logical:** *Just because I don't like his behaviour, how does it logically follow that this is a purposeful act?* **Pragmatic:** *Does holding on to this idea make my life better or worse?*	**Anger**	**Empirical:** *There is no evidence that he did this on purpose. Mention it to him but keep calm and find out the facts.* **Logical:** *I don't like being pushed in on. However, there is no logic in making a fuss but it is OK to point out what could be an innocent error.* **Pragmatic** *Even if I find it hard it is not the end of the world.*	If I mention what has happened, I am taking appropriate action. However, it is better to check out the facts first as this could be a simple error and nothing more sinister. Even if it is, getting angry harms me, and in the grand scheme of things, being pushed in on is not the end of the world. Point out the error clearly and calmly.

Challenge your thoughts

Jumping to conclusions

Look for *evidence* to challenge your thinking. If you believe you *'always get things wrong'*, think about occasions when you *'got things right'*. Check out your thinking by asking people what they really think rather than simply acting on what you believe – your beliefs are only assumptions.

Over-generalization

Learn to be your own best friend. Ask yourself what you would say to a friend in the same position. Don't you think it is strange that we are often kinder to others than we are to ourselves?

Shoulds and musts

Use the idea of 'preference' versus 'absolutist' statements like 'should'. When you use 'should' you are really saying that the world and the people in it (including yourself) absolutely must behave a certain way. For example, *'I really would prefer to get things right all the time'* instead of *'I must not get things wrong'*. There is nothing wrong with wanting to do well or wanting others to do the things we would want. However, there is *no rule* that says other people should do what we want, or that just because we want something we should have it!

All or nothing

When you find yourself thinking in an extreme way, look for the middle route. For example, could you break the task down into stages? Did you manage to do some of what you set out to do? If so, give yourself credit for what you *have* done.

Mental filter

Challenge your filter by writing down three good things that have happened each day. Watch out and listen for positive comments and when you find yourself worrying about something someone has said, ask yourself if you are ignoring the positive comments.

Discounting the positive

When you tell yourself that what you have done doesn't count, stop and give yourself a pat on the back. Make a point of finding someone to speak to out loud about what you have done. For example, '*I am really pleased with the way I spoke up – I did not lose my temper but spoke in a reasonable and measured way, letting people know what I think but without overdoing it.*'

Emotional reasoning/labelling

When you call yourself a negative name like stupid, a failure, or no-good, ask yourself what you *really* mean. After all, what makes someone a failure? You can fail at something like an exam, but failing at something is not a failure. It does not discount the positive.

The 'Big I, little I' exercise below can be useful. Draw the outline of a large I (Figure 4). This Big I represents you – then fill in the I with lots of little I's, and these I's represent different parts of your personality. For example 'I am kind', 'I can cook', and 'I have a good sense of humour'.

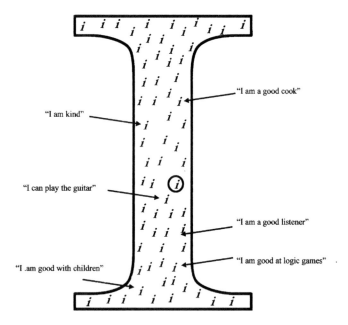

"I am a good cook"

"I am kind"

"I can play the guitar"

"I am a good listener"

"I am good at logic games"

"I .am good with children"

Figure 4. Big I, little I diagram

Personalization and blame

When you find yourself blaming yourself (or other
people) because you believe it is your entire fault, draw a
'responsibility pie' (see Figure 5). Think about all the
factors of the situation and how many people or circumstances have contributed to the outcome. As you carve up
the pie, you will see that you are only one part of a much
bigger system. Only take responsibility for what is yours,
learn from the situation for next time, and speak to others
about their part.

When you have worked out what actions belong to
whom, taking responsibility for what is yours and giving

back the responsibility that belongs to other people, allocate a percentage out of 100 to each of the people and/or areas you have identified.

Below are some useful questions that you can ask yourself.

What's the situation?

'I feel angry because my boss was upset with me or for not arriving on time to a meeting with a client. I explained that I had been held up because the train did not come on time but he still feels I let him down.'

What did you try to do?

I tried to ring on my mobile, but only got his voicemail. I tried ringing my assistant, but he did not answer his mobile. I did get through to the company we were visiting and left a message at reception.

What part do you think you played in the situation?

I could have left a little more time to get to the venue.

Me = thirty per cent

What part do other people or circumstances play?

My boss did change the time and I had to alter a number of my appointments to fit in. He did not check with me personally, but left a message on my voicemail and did not check to see if the change of time was convenient to me.

Boss = thirty per cent

There was an unexpected delay due to a signal failure.

Signal failure delayed train = forty per cent

Figure 5.   Ressponsibility pie chart

Catastrophizing

Notice the emotive language you are using and tone it down. Remember that things are not awful, a disaster, or a nightmare. This does not mean that the situation is not difficult, hard, or painful. Use words that put the situation into perspective. Ask yourself '*What's the worst that can really happen?*'

Life rules

Some people hold negative beliefs about themselves. For example, you may believe you are a failure, worthless, a bad person, stupid, unlovable, or unattractive. These beliefs shape your actions in everyday life. These beliefs can be seen as the rules that dictate the way we manage our daily lives.

An example of a life rule would be if you thought you were a failure and then spent your life confronting situations as a way of dealing with the fear of being found out. You may live your life believing that '*I must avoid being found out*', and that criticism from other people means you are in danger of being found out. '*My boss has suggested I try for a new role, but if I do I may fail the interview and then people will realize I am a failure*.' You may find yourself using your anger as a defence against the fear of being 'found out', or even against yourself, and avoid trying to change your situation, believing you are incapable of doing so because you are a failure and that it is not fair.

People whose life rules are about over-achieving as a way of fending off beliefs of failure tend to feel good only when they *are* achieving. If you believe yourself to be lacking in some way, you may believe that you are a worthless person because you do not conform to whatever you believe the standard to be. This also means that when things go wrong, which they invariably will do, you may find yourself feeling angry either at others, because you believe they are stopping you from achieving, or yourself for not managing to do as much as you think you should.

A person who believes she is only safe from her beliefs about failure may find herself feeling very angry if she is faced with a situation where she needs to prove herself in some way. Some people believe they are bad people and that if others really knew them, rather than the mask they present to the world, they would be disliked and seen as frauds. It is helpful to identify your basic beliefs so that you can use the counter-measures described in this book to change the ways you perceive yourself.

Beliefs about yourself, others, and the world have been formed by the messages you received from:

- family;
- friends;
- the world.

Over time you have been conditioned to think in a certain way and it takes time to change your belief, regardless of how motivated you are to do so.

Demands that may increase your anger

There are three types of demands we make of ourselves in the form of '*musts*' and these are:

Demands about self – e.g., '*I must always get it right*' (creates stress, anxiety, shame, and guilt).

Demands about others – e.g., '*You must behave well otherwise it is awful*' (creates anger).

Demands about the world – e.g., '*The world should be a fair and just place*' (creates self pity, addictive behaviour, and depression).

To help you identify your personal musts and the types of beliefs your musts are based on, write yourself an '*I must, otherwise I am*' list as follows.

Demands of self

I must_____ otherwise_____

e.g., I must be strong and capable, otherwise I am a failure.

Demands of others

You must_____ otherwise_____
e.g., *You must agree with me, otherwise I am wrong and that would be awful.*

Demands of the world

The world must_____ otherwise _____
e.g., *The world must treat me well if I work hard and do my best, otherwise it is not fair.*

When you have identified the personal demands you make of yourself, others, and the world, you need to set about challenging them. Do this in the same way you identified your automatic negative thoughts earlier.

Challenging your demands

You can challenge the demands you are making of yourself in the following ways:

- consider the impact your demand has on you and those around you;
- identify how you know when the demand is activated (i.e., the thoughts, feelings, and behaviours you experience);
- think about how the demand came about and the life experiences that sustain it;
- consider the advantages and disadvantages of holding on to your demand;
- identify a more appropriate way of rephrasing your demand, which fits with life as it is now;
- think about how you are going to put your new demand into action.

What if I can't identify a demand but suspect there is one?

Sometimes you find yourself saying things like, '*It would be awful*', or '*That's just not right*'. When you make statements like these it doesn't seem at first sight as if there is a core belief in operation. You could find a situation triggers a strong feeling and, although you identify your negative automatic thought and challenge it, you still seem to feel unhappy.

If this is the case, ask yourself a series of questions and, rather like an archaeological dig, these will help you uncover your core belief. It is sometimes helpful to see your thought at the beginning of a long chain and your core beliefs at the other end. You have to identify each link in the chain and, as you do so, you get nearer the end of the chain that holds your core belief.

For example:

Situation: You are challenged by a colleague at a meeting who does not believe that your idea is a good one.

Feeling: Anger

Thought: My idea is sound, and what right have you got to challenge me?

1. *Ask yourself*: '*What is so awful about being challenged?*'
    Answer: '*It means she does not have faith in me and respect the knowledge I have.*'

2. *Ask yourself*: '*Supposing that were true, what would that mean?*'
    Answer: '*It would mean that she thought I was stupid.*'

3. *Ask yourself: 'And if she did think I was stupid, what would that mean?'*
    Answer: *'People would laugh at me.'*

4. *Ask yourself: 'And if they did?'*
    Answer: *'That would be awful.'*

5. *Ask yourself: 'What would be awful?'*
    Answer: *'They would think I was not capable.'*

6. *Ask yourself: 'Suppose they did think I wasn't capable?'*
    Answer: *'They would know how dumb I am so I have to defend myself.'*

7. *Ask yourself: 'So what does being seen as dumb mean to me?'*
    Answer: *'I must never be seen as dumb otherwise this means I am a failure.'*

You end up with a core belief that, in this case, is *'I must defend myself against people challenging my ideas, otherwise I will be seen as dumb and this will mean I am a failure'*.

Summary

One way of looking at the role self-defeating thinking plays in shaping your life is to consider the relationship between automatic thoughts, demands/life rules, and core beliefs. Core beliefs are the conclusion you draw about yourself as a person, such as thinking you are basically bad, worthless, or a failure.

Automatic thoughts are triggered by the situations you find yourself in; for example, being asked to do something you do not want to do but thinking '*How dare they, I should not be asked to do this*'. Another way of thinking about demands is to see them as 'if–then' rules. For example, '*If I don't stand up for myself, then people will walk all over me.*' Core beliefs are absolutist beliefs we hold about ourselves, such as, '*I did not win that argument, which means I am a failure*'.

A simple way of thinking of this three-stage model is outlined in Figure 6.

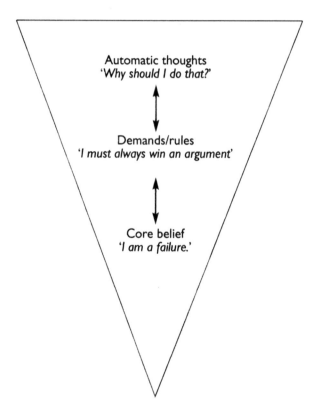

Figure 6.   Three-stage model of core beliefs.

The role of inhibitors

Society sets many rules about how an individual should behave and what is expected and these could be called *external inhibitors*. For example, you will often hear people talk about dealing with a petty official such as a security guard and how cross they were with the way they were dealt with, but that they chose to keep calm and not say what they really thought because they realized that by doing so they were less likely to get a positive outcome to their request since, whether they thought the response was reasonable or not, the person had the power to make life more difficult if they chose to. In such a situation you might feel unhappy, but would inhibit yourself from giving full reign to your thoughts, feelings, and actions because you would be thinking about the consequences of doing so. There are many times in life when an individual may fantasize about slashing someone's car tyres, but does not actually do so because that would lead to criminal charges, and this type of external inhibitor stops you from turning your fantasy into a reality.

There are also *internal inhibitors*, which are based more on how you see yourself and wish others to see you. For example, you may not like the way that a woman at a party flirts with your boyfriend. However, you choose to take it all in your stride and not to make a fuss, as you believe that to do so would make a scene and that you would come out of it looking bad in some way. Here, your desire to be seen positively by others overrides your desire to act on your feelings.

Inhibitors can be external or internal, and sometimes a mixture of both. For example, not slashing the tyres because you might get found out and would not like the consequences (external inhibitor) is linked with your thoughts that if you did this, it would make you look petty and you would not like to perceived in this way (internal inhibitor).

For people who are able to control or deal with their feelings of frustration or anger, inhibitors play a vital role in helping to moderate behaviour. Inhibitors are linked with 'life rules' – if you have a life rule that states '*If I am to be seen as reasonable then I need to follow the rules*', you are more likely to think about both the external and internal inhibitors in a situation. However, if your life rule is '*If someone does me down then I have to pay them back*', you are more likely to allow your anger to get the better of you as it becomes more important to 'pay someone back' than it is to follow the rules or be seen in a certain way.

Putting it all together – a model for understanding your anger

Figure 7 provides you with a model for understanding and analysing your feelings of irritability and anger.

The concept of good moods and bad moods

Having completed the exercises above you will probably begin to see that you can change the way you think about situations, and by doing this you can change your feelings, and your actions will, as a consequence, also be different.

The 'mood' we are in also very often has an impact on how we behave. For example, if I am unwell or tired I am

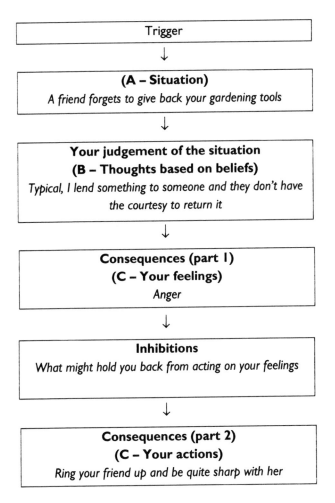

Figure 7. A model for understanding and analysing your anger

likely to be affected by situations more negatively than if I am rested and well. If things are not going so well for me on a personal level, this may also influence how I react, and I may be more irritable than I normally would be.

You could say that the 'mood' I am in will either help or hinder me in the way I deal with situations. However, I also have choices about how I can shape my own moods by choosing to think about what I am thinking and why, and to change the way I feel by changing the way I think. As we saw earlier all kinds of things can affect our mood – sleep, stress, alcohol, etc. Therefore, if it is possible for you to be in a 'good mood' one day and let things wash over you, then it is possible for you to re-create that mood, or at least modify your 'bad mood' so that it does not damage you or anyone else.

Table 5 is an example of a mood table.

Table 5. Mood table

Situation	Good mood	Bad mood
	I think . . .	I think . . .
Party going on two doors down with loud music.	*Nice to hear people enjoying themselves, can't remember the last time they had a party.*	*How inconsiderate – don't they realize what the time is?*
Children playing in the field at the back of the estate.	*The children are having a good time and it's nice that they have somewhere to play that is safe.*	*Why can't the parents take them to the park? They are making too much noise.*
Colleagues going out to lunch together.	*They are a nice bunch and will have some fun.*	*Typical, so much to do and all they can do is take time out.*

EXERCISE

1. Think of three situations that you find yourself in where, depending on your mood, you may see things completely differently, and complete the mood table below.

Mood table

Situation	Good mood I think . . .	Bad mood I think . . .

(continued)

> 2. Now that you have identified the three situations, look at what you have written down in relation to your 'bad mood' and identify which types of faulty thinking you engage in when you think this way. Once you have done this, look at your 'good mood' and identify what type of thinking makes you respond in a more positive way.

When you have completed the exercise you will see more clearly how good moods and bad moods are based on what we are thinking at the time. If you see thinking as a kind of self-talk, then if you can talk yourself into a bad mood you can talk yourself out!

Learn to accept yourself

The tips on the pages that follow are based on the principles of a therapy called Rational Emotive Behaviour Therapy, or REBT for short. You need to learn to like yourself, and to do this you need to accept yourself. They offer practical suggestions and ways to begin the process of self-acceptance. Self-acceptance is the arduous process of learning to like yourself 'warts and all'. Self-acceptance helps you to decrease your anger and increase your confidence.

Tips to help you like yourself

● Remember that human beings are not perfect and that *includes you*! There is no such thing as a person who is 100% right, good, capable, or strong. If you spend your life believing that perfection exists you will always be disappointed, unhappy, stressed, and in danger of being anxious and depressed. There is nothing wrong with wanting to do things well; be a good worker, student, parent, partner, or friend. Set yourself realistically high but not impossibly perfectionist standards.

- Remember that everyone is equal, regardless of ability. It is possible for someone to have greater talents or skills than you without being a *better person*. Stop comparing yourself to other people, as this can only lead to feelings of anxiety, resentment, or disappointment. If you admire someone for something they have done, there is nothing wrong with thinking about the quality they possess or the way they did something, trying to identify the key components so you can model your behaviour on theirs and learn from what they have done. Modelling yourself is not the same as comparing yourself. There may be differences in what people can do, but there is no difference in the basic worth of each human being. One person is not 'better' than another.

- There is no such thing as a 'global rating' on human goodness or badness. No one is ever *all good* or *all bad*. Good people sometimes do bad things and bad people sometimes do good things. If you behave in a way that later you think better about, then take the appropriate action. For example: apologise, explain, and see what you can do to put things right. However, doing something you later regret does not make you a bad person, just as doing one good deed does not make someone a saint. If you keep on seeing yourself and/or others in this all or nothing way, you place unrealistic pressure on yourself and on others.

- Over-generalization (see p. 63) is where you exaggerate one aspect of your behaviour (e.g., *'Because I allowed someone to win an argument, that makes me weak.'*). If you want to conquer your anger, it is important that you do not judge the *whole* of you on just one *part* of your behaviour; for example, *'I may not have got all that I wanted but I did get some of what I wanted.'* Keep things in proportion. Blowing things out of proportion wastes time and energy. Confident people deal with situations.

- Remember to work on dropping the *shoulds* and *musts,* as all they do is lead you to develop a conditional outlook on yourself. Dropping *shoulds, musts,* and *have tos* does not mean abdicating your responsibilities – it simply means stopping putting yourself down.

- Remember that self-acceptance is hard work. It requires energy and commitment and consistent work to make it happen.

You also need to:

- Learn to respect yourself – you are as valuable as everyone else

- Live a lifestyle that is supportive of your health – there is no point making yourself ill from overwork or abusing your body. Why be angry when you know that anger causes harm to you and to others? If you do this you are likely to increase your anger. For example, caffeine products are likely to increase your susceptibility to anger. Caffeine is a stimulant and, as people who are angry produce stress hormones (as we saw earlier under the section on stress response), stimulants such as caffeine help to increase the production of these hormones.

- Engage in supportive relationships and carry out the life audit that follows. Work at your relationships, make sure you have a variety and cultivate them as you would your garden plants. Tending to friendships pays you back tenfold with the love and concern others will feel and show towards you.

- Set goals for yourself specifically designed to improve your life and diminish your anger. When you undertake your annual life audit, set yourself a series of goals for the year. Decide what you want to change and how you will do it. The changes that you make and what you learn about yourself all go towards you developing new life skills and increasing your confidence.

- Recognize that change cannot be achieved overnight and that you will need to keep on working at challenging negative attitudes about yourself. I know this has been said more than once, but that's because it is so important.

- Spend time and money on yourself – you are worth it! Learn to pamper yourself. Many people's anger is increased because of the way they drive themselves, therefore taking time out and enjoying life is a way of countering this tendency.

- Remember that you need to take responsibility for your own life. It is all too easy to blame other people or 'bad luck' for situations. However bad your situation, you *do* have choices. Sometimes you have to give yourself what I call a 'therapeutic kick up the backside'. When things go wrong it is helpful to allow yourself to feel your feelings, to express your emotions appropriately and to seek support from others. It is not helpful to spend time raging about how things should be, as this will not change the situation and is likely to make it worse rather than better.

Ask yourself if there is a payoff for continuing to engage in a particular behaviour. For example, if you allow others to make all the decisions for you, the payoff may be that you never have to face 'being in the wrong', and you can always blame them for the way things have turned out.

Learn to appreciate yourself

Often, to the outside world, angry people appear arrogant, and yet the person concerned may perceive him or herself negatively and be lacking in confidence. Many outwardly aggressive people are in fact highly sensitive and easily hurt, with a poor self-image.

If you have been lacking in confidence for a long time, you may find it hard to identify and appreciate your good points. Go back to page 69 and complete the 'Big I, Little I' exercise, if you have not done so already. If you need more help, ask yourself the following questions.

- What am I able to do?
- What do I like about myself?
- What have I learnt in life?
- How would someone else describe me?
- How will I ensure I actually practise these skills – what might get in the way?

The life audit

The life audit is a technique to help you identify the areas of your life you would benefit from changing. A life audit should be undertaken on an annual basis, with quarterly 'check-ups' to monitor progress.

A life audit is a way of working out what in life you are happy with, need to get more of, or need to stop doing. Once you have completed the audit itself, the next step is to set about making changes to those areas of your life you have identified as needing attention. There is no point working out what you like or dislike unless you are prepared to change the things you are unhappy about and increase the things you like. People who suffer from anger very often just let life happen – although they may scream and shout they may not do anything productive to change their situation. The life audit is one way for you to take up that control.

EXERCISE

Write down all the things you like and dislike about each of the following eight areas of your life:

- Living environment (e.g., *flat, house, geographical area*)
- Family (e.g., *family of origin, children*)
- Personal relationship(s) (e.g., *partner*)
- Friends/social life (e.g., *friendships, hobbies, outings*)
- Work/career (e.g., *current job, future aspirations*)
- Finances (e.g., *budgeting, savings, pensions, investments*)
- Health (e.g., *diet, exercise, stress management*)
- Inner soul/spirit (e.g., *your sense of purpose in life*)

Example – life audit

Work/career

Like	Dislike
Having an influence on outcome	*The long hours*
Meeting new people	*Journey to the office*
Good perks	

Consider each of the things you don't like and ask yourself what you could do to change the situation. Research suggests that you are far more likely to carry out your plans if you write them down.

Action plans

Work/career

Dislike	Action plan
Long hours	Other people manage to leave the office and are still well thought of. Perhaps I am making life harder than it need be and I could leave the office earlier than I do at least for three nights a week.

Distraction

Distraction techniques are helpful when you are angry and keep having thoughts that are making you feel uncomfortable or are undermining your efforts. Distraction is a way of taking your attention away from what is happening on to something else. When you find yourself beginning to feel angry, you need to decide not to think about your thoughts and then engage your mind with something else. Have you ever found yourself in the position of beginning to experience a sense of frustration only to find that something happened to distract you and your feeling changed?

There are three types of distraction:

1. Paying attention to what is going on around you – try guessing the ages of people in the room or listen to someone else's conversation, or decide to count as many round objects as you can see in the room.
2. Physical activity – try cleaning, tidying up, or finding tasks to do.
3. Engage in some form or mental activity – recite your times tables, say the alphabet backwards, or do a crossword.

ANGER-FREE EMOTIONS

Learn to be emotionally smart

Emotional intelligence is about learning to being emotionally smart. It is not always the person with the highest IQ who does best. Emotionally smart people get the most from managing their own and other people's emotions. If you can learn the skills of emotional smartness it will help you overcome your anger. When you are angry you may find that people do not listen to what you have to say because they are too busy reacting to your anger. They may decide not to consult you because they do not want to antagonize you and deal with the fall-out. They may talk about you behind your back and you may get a reputation as someone who is difficult.

The skills fall into five key areas.

Identifying your emotions

Emotionally smart people are able to identify their own emotions. This means learning to tell other people how you feel. It means taking responsibility for your own emotions by starting sentences with '*I feel . . .*'

Managing your emotions

Emotions can be difficult, and emotionally smart people know when to take care of themselves. For example, when you find things difficult what are the things you do to take care of yourself? Do you have a long hot bath and relax? Do you talk to a friend? Do you get a DVD or video and

---

EXERCISE

How to identify emotions

1. Look at the series of positive and negative words below. Place a tick against the words you think describe you best.
2. Why have you chosen those particular words?
3. If you were to change your negative words to positive ones, what would you have to do?

Positive	Negative
Empathic	Angry
Loving	Anxious
Happy	Jealous
Joyful	Possessive
Caring	Remorseful
Enthusiastic	Envious
Warm	Resentful

EXERCISE

Taking care of my emotions

List two ways in which you take care of yourself and two ways in which you take care of other people (e.g., warm bath, ring a friend, encourage someone to talk).

Me	Others
1.	1.
2.	2.

watch that? There are times when you need to take care of other people's emotions and there are times when you need to motivate yourself and others.

Other people's emotions

Emotionally smart people have developed the ability to pick up other people's emotions. Using skills such as empathy (the ability to imagine what it might feel like to see the world from another perspective), a smart person considers how the other person might be feeling, realizing that such recognition can encourage a more co-operative relationship.

EXERCISE

How do I show my understanding of others?

Think about people and situations where you feel a connection with what the person is feeling. This ability of being able to imagine what it is like for the other person is called empathy. Choose friends or use characters from films or television. Think about why you empathize with the person you have chosen.

Those I empathize with	*Reasons I empathize with them*
_____	_____
_____	_____
_____	_____
_____	_____

(*continued*)

Now, list all the ways in which you would demonstrate your understanding to another person (e.g., *giving the person my full attention or using certain words*).

_____

_____

_____

_____

_____

Learning to motivate yourself

There are times when strong emotions get in the way. There may be times when it is better to put off your own needs and wants for a future pay-off. Some people find themselves so caught up in their immediate emotions that they forget there is a bigger picture.

EXERCISE

When have I motivated myself or others?

Think of two situations where you have motivated yourself or other people. In particular, think of situations where there has been strong emotion. How did you cope with the strong emotion so that you were able to complete the task in hand?

Situation 1

What happened?

(continued)

What I did:

Situation 2

What happened?

What I did:

Healthy relationships

Life is full of relationships, so it makes sense to consider the behaviours that help to create happy and productive relationships while recognizing those that destroy them.

EXERCISE

Ways of creating positive relationships

List three ways to cultivate a relationship (e.g., ringing people regularly, remembering special events, or listening to a friend's problems)

1.

2.

3.

Learning to appreciate yourself and others

How do you feel when I ask you to:

> list five things you could do better;
> list five things that have gone well and you are pleased with?

I suspect you found the first question easier to answer and the second more difficult. Most people neglect the power of praise and appreciation – the bottom line is that appreciation and praise motivate.

Some people fear that if they praise themselves or others, it will lead to a slacking off in effort or that they will be seen as weak. It is well documented that children who are constantly criticized are more likely to have poor confidence and to stop trying to improve. They may even feel angry about getting things wrong.

Success encourages success and every time you or someone else does something well (even partially well) it is one more step towards building an anger-free life.

EXERCISE

Past praise

The last time I praised myself was . . .

1. _____

_____

_____

(continued)

Present praise

Think of two things that you can praise yourself for and complete the following sentences.

I am pleased with myself because _____

_____

I think I have done well to _____

_____

EXERCISE

Your epitaph

Use the following space to write your own epitaph. How would you like to be remembered? I've written one as an example of what one could look like.

He knew what he wanted and always tried to get it, but he was a fair and reasonable man that people respected.

Write yours here.

_____

_____

_____

_____

When you wrote your epitaph what feelings came up for you? Look at what you have written and consider whether you are living your life in a way that is likely to make your words come true. What changes do you need to make and how will you set about making those changes?

Other people's emotions

If you have the ability to read and understand other people's emotions, you have a great advantage in influencing people's attitudes towards you.

Reading emotions means:

1. *Watching body language*
   People's body language and voice tone tell you a lot about how they are feeling and your body language is also a way of communicating. Angry people often try to overpower others – they stare at people, raise their voices, and look menacing, sometimes invading another person's space.

2. *Listening to the words*
   What do the words tell you? Sometimes people tell you what they are feeling (e.g., *I feel cross about what you have just said*). If you think of the words you use, what impact do you think they have? What do they say about you?

3. *Using your empathy*
   Empathy, as we explored earlier, is the ability to imagine what it might be like to see the world wearing someone else's shoes. Empathy can be expressed through statements such as '*You sound frustrated*', and '*I imagine you were very unhappy about that*'.

How to deal with strong emotion

Strong emotions can be disturbing for both the person experiencing them and for those around at the time. Many people feel uncomfortable with expressing emotions or being around people who are expressing them.

Strong emotions could include anxiety, anger, or severe emotional distress. Sometimes you may be frightened by the strength of the emotion you feel; for example, being overwhelmed with anger. Being around an angry person can be difficult as anger can often be felt by others and this can either make the other person feel anxious or make them cut the contact short as they find it an uncomfortable emotion.

It is easier to handle strong emotions if you make a point of acknowledging them. If you suppress feelings, never admitting them to yourself or others, they get stored. Sooner or later there is simply too much stored emotion, the natural suppression mechanism stops working, and a sudden outpouring takes place.

Some people believe they should let all their emotions show all the time. These people lack emotional intelligence, as they influence other people's attitudes towards them by being overly dramatic and emotional.

There are, of course, times when strong emotions are understandable; for example, if you had just had bad news or if you needed to defend yourself against violent attack.

Exercise

When was the last time you felt a strong emotion?

Think of the last time you experienced a strong emotion – what had happened? What did you feel? How did you deal with your emotion and what was the outcome? When you have completed the exercise, look at your reactions and ask yourself whether you are happy with what you did. If you are not happy, what could you have done differently?

What actually happened:

What I felt at the time:

What I did at the time:

Outcome:

What could I have done differently?

_____

_____

_____

_____

_____

Don't put things off!!!

Anger is overcome by tackling life head on as much as you can. Make a list of all the things you have put off. Procrastination tends to compound problems. The more you mean to do but never get around to doing the more your anger is likely to grow. If you have a lot of things on your list you cannot do them all at once, so why not rate them in terms of difficulty, for example by using a scale of 0–10:

0   1   2   3   4   5   6   7   8   9   10
(0 = easy and 10 = really hard)

Examples:
Taking up yoga   = 3
Handling a difficult conversation   = 5
Returning goods to a shop   = 7

Once you have drawn up this list, start with items that have a rating of between three and seven. Anything rated more than a seven may be too difficult for you at the beginning of the process. Conversely, anything less than a three may be too easy.

Always remember to praise yourself on your achievements. Think about *what you have* managed to do rather than what you believe you *should* have been doing. Keeping this kind of a record provides you with evidence of the goals you have set and your success in dealing with them.

Everyone has bad days, days when you feel that nothing has been achieved or changed. By keeping these details in your journal you have a written record of the improvements you have made and these help you evaluate your progress realistically.

Get moving

In addition to exercise being physically healthy, it is also good for our psychological well-being. Research suggests that even mild exercise can have a positive effect. Simply walking a couple of miles each day and walking up and down stairs can do the trick. Exercise not only relieves stress, it also releases naturally produced chemicals which can raise your mood and help you find an outlet for pent-up emotion. A number of people who are prone to anger find that exercise has a calming effect.

Guilt

Some people who are angry also feel guilty. We often say that we feel guilty, but guilt is not so much a feeling as a thought process. When you say you feel guilty it usually means:

- you have broken one of your value rules, e.g., '*I must always be strong and know what to do*'.
- you think only about the outcome of what you believe you have done or not done, e.g., '*I should not have shouted at my daughter*'.

These types of guilt are either about the *actions you have taken*, or the *choices you have made*, and the consequences of your choices. A value rule is part of the moral code by which you live your life, whereas an outcome is more about what you have done.

There are some people who believe they are guilty simply because they are alive. Someone who feels guilty, but cannot tell you why, may experience this kind of guilt. This type of guilt stays with such people throughout life unless they change the way they think about themselves and the world.

If you've made a mistake, it makes sense to put it right. Try to do something to put the situation right. If you simply feel guilty without taking action, you are likely to avoid people, places, and activities that remind you of the guilt you feel.

You can deal with guilt by:

- asking yourself what you actually feel guilty about;
- asking yourself if you were to find yourself in exactly the same situation today would you behave any differently;
- thinking about the way your core beliefs influence the way you live your life and whether it is possible for anyone to live up to all of those core beliefs all of the time;
- remembering *'bad things happen to good people and good people sometimes do bad things'*.
- examining your 'thinking style' for examples of the kind of self-defeating thoughts described earlier (p. 66);
- remembering that you are a fallible human being;
- realizing that if there is something you can do to change the situation for others, then doing so;
- not hiding away from the world – it won't make things better just make you feel worse;
- learning to forgive yourself and remembering that forgiveness is a choice.

Use the 'Big I, Little I' (p. 69) to remind yourself of your positive points and use the 'Responsibility pie' (p. 72) to help you work out who is responsible for what.

Cost–benefit analysis

It can be hard to change your behaviour, particularly if you have been acting in a certain way for a long time. A 'cost–benefit analysis' can help you identify the costs and the benefits of behaving in a certain way.

Use the cost–benefit sheet below to work out what is happening. You can write down all the benefits of continuing to act the way you are on the right-hand side of the page. Then on the left-hand side of the page you write down all the costs (emotional and practical) of continuing as you are. An example is shown below.

Cost–benefit analysis model
Name: John Angry   Date: 10/10/05
Situation: *I have to be right at all costs*

COST	BENEFIT
<ul><li>Feel agitated</li><li>Other people are nervous around me and treat me with caution</li><li>I often feel bad about the way I have behaved</li><li>I am not progressing well in my career because I tend to give a poor impression of myself</li><li>I have lost partners because of my behaviour</li></ul>	<ul><li>I sometimes get what I want</li></ul>

Now complete your own analysis.

My cost–benefit analysis	
Name: Date: Situation:	
COST	BENEFIT

Once you have completed both sides of the form you will be in a better position to make decisions about what you want to do. If you want to change you need to decide what you need to do.

The role of assertiveness

Assertiveness means asking for what you want and saying what you feel, while respecting the needs and rights of others. Many people think that being assertive is rather like being in the SAS – you take no prisoners. This is not the case. Anyone who thinks like this has aggression mixed up with assertion. Some people also think that assertiveness training is only useful to people who are passive and anxious. However, this is very far from the truth, as assertiveness training is also of tremendous value to people who experience anger as their primary way of dealing with situations. What assertion training does is to provide you with the tools and strategies that you need to be able to deal with situations calmly, thoughtfully, and in a way that gives you the best chance of getting what you want out of a situation in the best possible way.

The more assertive you become, the more you come to realize that 'compromise' is not a dirty word and that people who compromise get more of what they want from the world around them. People who are angry often see every situation as one of either 'win or lose', and yet most of life is about finding a middle way.

Truly assertive people look for what is called a 'win-win' situation and take responsibility for their own actions. Becoming more assertive improves the way we can communicate with others. Most colleges and evening institutes are likely to offer short courses on assertiveness. There is more about assertion in the next section – 'Anger-Free Actions'.

Shame and humiliation

You can feel shame because you believe you have broken one of your value rules – one you hold about yourself or one you believe about others. If you believe you have behaved in a way frowned on by friends, family, or society you may feel shame. You may remember the term catastrophizing from the 'Anger-Free Thinking' section of this book. You tell yourself that it is 'awful' you feel a certain thing or have behaved in a certain way. 'Awfulizing' is often expressed in terms of criticism about personal weakness . . . *'If people thought I was weak then that would be awful. People would think less of me'*.

People who experience shame have a great capacity for avoiding people and places that remind them of what they see as their weakness.

Humiliation usually means you believe you have lost status in some way. Humiliation is closely linked to the same kind of thought processes that are associated with shame and guilt, in particular around the issue of worrying about how others will somehow think less of you as a result of your loss of status.

How to deal with shame and humiliation

You can ask yourself:

- do I really believe someone thinks less of me as a result of what I have done and, if so, why? (Remember to use the skills you have learnt in the 'Anger-Free Thinking' section of this book.)
- Would I think less of someone who had gone through an identical experience?

If you have answered 'no' to both questions, why hold yourself responsible when you would not treat others the same way?

Dealing with worry

Angry people worry just as much as, and sometimes more than, other people. So many people worry about every aspect of life. Anger, as we saw earlier, can be based on fear. Things go wrong and there will be times when you are worried. For example, if your child were unwell then it would be normal for you to have some concern regarding the outcome. The whole area of fear can be rated in terms of mild, moderate, or severe feelings. Mild fear could be seen as worry, whereas severe fear could be seen as terror. Anger can also be rated as mild, moderate, or severe and an individual's reactions to each of these stages could range from being mildly irritated to moderately frustrated to full-blown raging.

How to worry constructively

Think about the following:

- 39% of the things you worry about never happen;
- 32% of things you worry about have already happened;
- 21% of your worries are over trivialities;
- 9% of your worries relate to important issues where you have legitimate cause for concern.

(Note: a total of 101% due to rounding up.)

If we stopped worrying it would not be helpful, as a certain amount of concern can help you think through what you could do and provides you with the opportunity of being cautious so that you can explore all the options to come up with the best course of action.

Your worry notebook

Take any notebook and divide it into four sections using the headings shown in the example below.

WORRIES FOR TODAY

1. **Things of concern that might happen**	2. **Insignificant things**
I have the roofer coming over to check the roof as rain has started to come in, and I am worried he will find more wrong than I think there is.	*I might be a little late to work this week as there are some problems on the trains, although there is no real problem about this as I have nothing important to do and everyone knows about the issue to do with the trains.*
3. **Things that have happened**	4. **Important things**
I did not handle a client meeting as well as I could have.	*There is talk that the firm might merge with another and this could have an implication for my role.*

Make the entries for headings 1, 2, and 3 before you go to bed. Choose the time of day you are at your strongest and brightest to complete section 4.

When it comes to section 4, you need to remember that *worrying about a problem does not solve it – doing something about it does.* If you do not make a decision to do something positive you can end up making a decision by default. No action still has an outcome. You need to decide whether you want to be in control (as much as is possible), or if you are going to just let things happen. There is *always* a choice.

Relaxation

When you feel angry it is useful to do some of the relaxation exercises mentioned earlier. There are many forms of relaxation, as we discussed, and some require physical movement while others require nothing more than breathing or visualization techniques.

How to use coping imagery to deal with negative emotions

According to research, when you visualize a positive outcome you are more likely to get one. Coping imagery is used as a way of preparing yourself for events.

EXERCISE

If you do not have a current or future situation that causes you concern then think about the last one that did.

- First, write out a 'problem list' of all the people, places and situations you feel uncomfortable with or in. Use the 0–10 scale as a way of rating the degree of discomfort you feel (0 = no discomfort and 10 = maximum discomfort).

- Once you have made out your list, choose something that has a rating of no more than seven. (Choosing a higher rating would make it too difficult and choosing a lower rating would not be challenging enough.) After all, you want to succeed, and if you make your task too difficult you may set yourself up to fail.

(continued)

- Now, close your eyes and imagine yourself at the beginning of your task. Use all your senses to imagine the sights, the sounds, and the smells. Think about what you would say and what you would do. Think about what you think the other person(s) might say. Use coping strategies like breathing, anchoring, and helpful self-talk to help you deal with the event.
- Now practise this visualization two or three times, each time seeing yourself coping with the situation. You may find that practising this exercise actually reduces your original rating, even though you are using only your imagination. It is as if your brain is fooled into believing that you really *have done* whatever you set out to do. Once you have practised this exercise a few times the next task is actually to do it!

Maximum benefit is gained from the above technique when you practise it frequently.

If you find it hard to use your imagination, try the following exercise to improve your visualization skills and develop your imagination 'muscles'. Like everything else in life, with practice, your ability will improve.

- Imagine looking at the sky at night.
- Choose one star and watch it become brighter and then dimmer. Do this repeatedly.
- See if you can track the star across the sky.

ANGER-FREE ACTIONS

Graded exposure

If you want to overcome your anger you have to challenge your behaviour. Anger makes us behave in ways that are not helpful, and when you give in to your feelings all you do is give power to the anger. Also, you may well find that as your anger increases, your positive outcomes become less favourable. For example, you are on the phone to arrange for someone to come out and repair your hands-free car phone system and the call does not go the way you think it should do. You have given them a lot of information but, because you have not got the response you think you should have, you end up slamming the phone down and then having to ring back and start all over again with someone else as the agent was at a call centre where many people are answering calls.

If you really want to conquer your anger, you need to engage in what is called graded exposure, which means that you start to face those situations you find difficult by engaging a range of coping strategies to help you deal with your feelings. Research has shown that when you face a difficult situation your feelings will peak, and if you can stay in the situation the feelings will come down to a more bearable level.

There are four stages to using graded exposure.

Stage one

Make a list of all the situations you find difficult to deal with without getting angry. Then, using a scale of 0–8

113

(0 = no anger; 8 = extreme anger), rate each of the items on the list.

Stage two

Now that you have rated the items, place them in order of degree of difficulty.

Stage three

You may want to select the easiest item on your list as the first one to start with. One word of advice here though – it is probably best to start with an item you have rated at four. If you try to deal with anything more than a four, it may be too difficult for you to manage. If you start with an item rated less than four, it may be too easy. An item rated four is hard enough for you to get the benefit of the exercise in terms of stretching yourself, but not so high that it is asking too much of you.

Stage four

Plan how you will tackle your task and what coping strategies you will use; for example, breathing, having a coping statement that you will repeat to yourself, or using distraction. Repeat this activity as many times as it takes for you to manage it without difficulty.

When you have successfully dealt with this item, go back to your list and move on to the next item.

The trick with graded exposure is that you must undertake the tasks regularly and for prolonged periods of time, so that the anger passes and you become more proficient at using your coping strategies.

Sometimes progress may seem slow and you may want to give up. However, progress is progress and giving up will only make matters worse, as by doing so you will convince yourself that you will never change. One small step at a time is still a step in the right direction. Do not discount what you have achieved. Learning to recognize your achievements, however small you think they are, is a way of increasing your confidence. When you find yourself 'discounting the positives', using statements such as '*So what, anyone could do this*', say to yourself '*I managed to handle that situation better than I would have normally and I managed to stay calmer than usual for some of the time*'.

Using coping imagery to reduce anger

Dealing with angry feelings is not easy, and you will need a range of coping strategies from changing the way you think about situations to calming your body down by breathing. In addition, you can also use imagery as a way of helping yourself to manage your feelings and the situations you may face.

An imagery technique helps to prepare you for the event as a way to help decrease your anger and practise the type of coping strategies that might be helpful. When anger levels have fallen to four or five, using your rating scale, it might be the time to consider tackling the task you have set yourself.

Coping imagery requires a person to imagine him or herself coping in a situation that usually causes them to become angry. The following describes the sequence of action for dealing with a specific situation, say dealing with questions at the weekly meeting held at your office, where you tend to see the questions asked of you as criticism and therefore react negatively and with increasing anger at them.

1. First, write out a 'fears list', outlining a hierarchy of difficult situations associated with your weekly meeting using a scale of 0–8.

   Consider the Peter's list as an example.

   Thinking about attending the meeting =3

   Waiting for my turn to speak about my items=4
   Speaking about my agenda items   =5
   Listening to the first comment   =7
   Having a colleague continue to question me =8

2. Once you have your own list made out, choose something that has a rating of no more than four or five. (Choosing anything with a higher rating would make it too difficult. A rating lower than two would probably not be challenging enough.)

   (Peter decided to take waiting for his turn to speak about his agenda item, that he rated as a four. He then went on to imagine the following.)

3. Now, close your eyes and imagine yourself sitting in the meeting. Use all your senses to imagine the people, the sights (room), and smells (coffee). Imagine yourself watching your colleagues talking about other items on the agenda and monitor the feeling you are experiencing. Use coping strategies like breathing, anchoring, and helpful self-talk while you imagine yourself dealing with these feelings in a helpful manner.

(Peter had already been taught how to relax through breathing, and had anchored a pleasant memory to a watch he always wore. He knew how his body worked, when angry, in releasing stress hormones into the system, and that apart from irritation he also felt anxious about dealing with the comments well and appearing competent. He had also put together some helpful self-talk such as 'I know the reasons behind my comments and they are sound; I question other people about their ideas and this does not mean I think any the less of them if I do not agree'.)

4. If you are using your coping strategies your anger is likely to abate, and once it has reduced to, say a three, you can choose something a little more difficult from the list you have drawn up.

Peter practised this exercise for two days, three times a day, until his anger had subsided to a three. Peter had a weekly meeting the following day and decided to repeat this exercise twice before that day, together with some breathing exercises before and during the meeting. He told himself that his only task for the meeting was to try to keep himself calmer while waiting for his turn, and that this is all he would focus on.

Peter found that the exercise went well, and although his anger went up to a five when sitting in the weekly meeting for real, it took very little time for it to subside. He used all his coping strategies and was very pleased with what he achieved. His success gave him the confidence to increase the degree of difficulty, using the items on his list.

To gain the maximum benefit from the above technique, you need to practise it frequently. Once you feel confident enough, you need to follow through with a real life event.

When you undertake a live exercise, you should use all the coping strategies you have practised in your imagination. It is also important to remember to break down your exercises into small, manageable steps. Trying to do too much will put too much strain on you and could lead to a sense of failure. Remember that old maxim '*success breeds success*'.

Remember, if you have difficulty visualizing and using your imagination, see the exercise at the end of page 112.

Problem-solving

Being able to deal with problems can help you manage your anger. Your thinking style, as we saw in the chapter on 'Anger-Free Thinking', affects how effectively you manage your life. Solving problems provides you with the chance of learning new skills.

One way of dealing with problems is to use the six-stage problem-solving model (Figure 8).

Six-stage problem-solving model

Stage one: identify the problem

The first step is to identify exactly what is wrong. When defining a problem, it is important to be as clear and specific as possible about what exactly is troubling you.

You identify the problem by:

- writing down what is happening, who is involved and what you believe is wrong. For example, *Situation*: been asked to meet with a difficult client. *Those involved*: two colleagues and me. *What is wrong*: this client always puts down anyone else's ideas and tends to change her own ideas throughout the meeting;

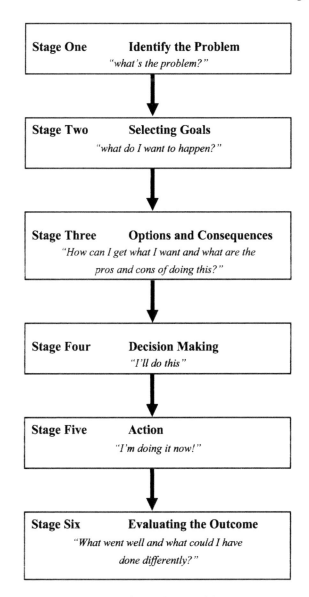

Figure 8.   The six-stage problem-solving model

- drawing a circle in the middle of a page to represent you, and then putting all the external and internal influences around you. For example, *an external influence* would be the actual information you need, whereas *an internal influence* might be *'feeling unsure of how to manage her constant changes'*.

Stage two: selecting goals

The next task is to set yourself a goal. Your goal needs to be specific. Although *'I want to manage the client meeting better than I normally do'* tells you what you want, it is not specific enough. A better alternative would be *'I want to answer this client's questions in a clear and calm manner'*. This example more clearly states what you want to do.

If you set yourself a goal you have to measure whether you are achieving it or not. Goals need to be specific and measurable as well as realistic. Are you one of those people who set themselves unrealistic goals? For example, *'I want to be able to answer all her questions'*. If you set yourself unrealistic goals you are likely to be discouraged and feel like a failure. Unless you are a mind reader, or have the questions in advance, you cannot know what she might ask, and no matter how hard or well you prepare it is possible that she may ask you something you cannot answer immediately but will have to research and/or think about.

The next step is to make sure your goal is relevant, and the last part of the goal-setting process is to set yourself a time limit. When are you meeting her and are the strategies you are employing going to help you remain calmer?

One way of remembering the goal-making process is to remember the acronym *SMART.*

S pecific:	Goals should be short and clear.
	e.g., *I want to answer this client's questions in a clear and calm manner.*
M easurable:	This considers how you will measure your progress.
	e.g., *I will ask my colleagues to help me out by getting them to provide me with a sign that I am achieving this in the meeting.*
A chievable:	Is your goal realistic?
	e.g., *If I practise my coping strategies and also base these on the information gained of the client at previous meetings then I am likely to handle the meeting in a more productive manner than I have done.*
R elevant:	How relevant is my goal?
	e.g., *The meeting will be more productive and I will feel more in control.*
T ime:	How much time should I allocate?
	e.g., *I have two weeks in which to prepare for the meeting.*

Stage three: options and consequences

OPTIONS

Once you have identified the problem you need to consider the associated consequences.

BRAINSTORMING

Brainstorming is one technique you can use to help you expand your options; it involves the following.

1. Writing down the issue at the top of the page.
2. Giving yourself ten minutes to come up with as many ideas as you can. As you write down your ideas you:
   - do not censor your ideas, regardless of how far-fetched you think they are;
   - go for quantity and not quality at this stage.
3. Once you have exhausted yourself in terms of your ideas, you can go back over them and see which ones seem useful and which ones you will disregard.

WHO CAN HELP YOU?

Perhaps you know someone who has dealt with a similar situation – how did they do it? If your problem is work-related, perhaps your organization offers a coaching scheme. If your problem is personal, you may have a friend or family member who can help.

CONSEQUENCES

Now that you have identified your options, you need to consider the pros and cons attached to each one. As in the cost–benefit analysis earlier, it is best to write everything down.

Brainstorming is a good tool for considering the consequences of a particular course of action. In an earlier chapter you were introduced to the power of imagery and using your imagination. You may wish to visualize your options and use your imagination to 'see' what could happen.

Stage four: decision making

Your plan may require one course of action or a series of actions. If you are unable to make a decision it may be because:

- it is impossible to solve the problem – maybe all that can be done is to manage the situation;
- you need more information;
- you are unclear about choosing between the various options available to you.

If you believe the problem is impossible to solve, try rewording it or breaking it down into smaller sections that are more easily resolved. If you require more information, you need to decide how to get this.

When you are confused between two or more options you may find it useful to talk to a friend or colleague. Use the rating scale (0–10) you were introduced to earlier to see if any of the options has the edge over another. Think about each option and try to visualize how you imagine things would be if you took that course of action.

HOW TO MANAGE SETBACKS

Although you have considered the pros and cons of a variety of actions, you may also find it useful to have a contingency plan worked out. A contingency plan means thinking about what to do if things do not go according to plan.

For example, if you wanted to write a report, what could get in the way of you completing it? How many things could go wrong, and how would you react to each of them? The 'Personal Contingency Plan' set out as Table 6 is a way of helping you think through and predict all the things that could go wrong, and how you would deal with such events if they occurred. Brainstorm as many problems as you can foresee before undertaking this exercise.

Table 6. Personal contingency plan
Feeling (rate 0–10)

What could go wrong?	What could I do if this happens?
1. *I might not have enough time to practise my coping strategies.*	*I need to mark out time in my diary on a daily basis to ensure I create the time.*
2. *I might not prepare as well as I could.*	2. *I need to make an outline of all the types of questions she could ask associated with this project and I can also ask my colleagues for ideas about what they think she might ask or areas she might want to change.*
3. *My feelings of anger might get the better of me.*	3. *If I use my breathing exercises and challenge my cognitions I will be able to manage my feelings better than I normally do.*
4.	4.
5.	5.
6.	6.

You may find that some of your plans of action require practice; for example, practising challenging unhelpful cognitions.

Stage five: action

Once you have made your decision you need to ensure you are fully resourced with everything you need to take action. You may find it helpful to keep a note of every action you take, together with the outcome. By completing an action plan you can tick off everything you have completed and see how each of your actions adds up to changing your situation. Some people find it helpful to place a series of reminders, or post-it notes, around the house, office, in a diary, and/or on the telephone. These post-it notes act as reminders for the things that need to be done.

Example

20 October 2005

1. Ring Jean and ask her for her ideas about the way she thinks the client may deal with the meeting and the items to be discussed.
2. Remember to practise my breathing exercise as this helps me stay calm.

Stage six: evaluating the outcome

You are the best judge of whether your problem is solved. Using the SMART goal-setting formula mentioned earlier makes it easier to measure your success. By making your goal specific, it is easier to see how far you have gone in achieving what you set out to do. Another way is to use what is called a 'continuum'; that is, a line that acts as a graded scale of how far you feel you have managed to come. Once you have drawn your line, place an X at the point that you believe most closely matches your progress.

Example

Losing my temper ———X———Staying calm

If you have achieved what you set out to do, then you can bring the problem-solving process to an end. If you have made no progress at all, you need to radically over-haul the steps you have taken and the decisions you have

125

made. You may, for example, have been rather ambitious in the goal you set yourself. It may have seemed feasible at the time, but you may have found the implementation more difficult than you anticipated. If this is the case, you need to go back to the beginning of the problem-solving process and, this time, break down the tasks into more manageable steps.

You may have identified more deep-rooted problems you feel you cannot tackle on your own, and you may require professional help. On those occasions where a partial completion of goals has been achieved, you need to consider what went well and what proved difficult. You may feel you are happy enough with what you have achieved, or you may feel that you need to take those aspects that you have been less successful with and set about a new problem-solving process with these.

Assertion training

Assertion training encourages people to use skills that build upon inner resources. Assertiveness aids clear communication with other people.

Assertiveness quiz

The following questions are designed to help you assess your behaviour patterns. Be honest in your responses and answer each question by writing the most appropriate letter in the box: Y for 'Yes', N for 'No', S for 'Sometimes', or N for 'Never'. Choose the response that most closely matches your behaviour.

1. Do you say what you feel?   ☐
2. Do you make decisions easily?   ☐
3. Are you critical of other people?   ☐
4. Do you say something if someone
   pushes in front of you?   ☐
5. Do you usually have confidence in
   your own decision-making capacity?   ☐
6. Do you lose your temper quickly?   ☐
7. Do you find it hard to say 'No'?   ☐
8. Do you continue with an argument
   after the other person has finished?   ☐
9. When you discover goods are faulty,
   do you take them back?   ☐
10. Do you feel shy in social situations?   ☐
11. Are you able to show your emotions?   ☐
12. Are you able to ask people for help?   ☐

Note: There is no right or wrong answer to the questions above. The answers that you have given provide you with information about your personal style of behaviour. You are now in a position to decide whether you are happy with the answers you have given and whether you would like to change the way that you behave.

Four types of behaviour

Non-assertive/passive

PERSONAL FEELINGS

A non-assertive person often feels helpless, powerless, inadequate, frustrated and lacking in confidence.

BEHAVIOURS

Signs of being passive:

- not asking for what you want;
- not saying what you feel;
- avoiding situations where you have to make decisions;
- feeling like a victim and/or martyr;
- finding it hard to say 'no' so that you become over-committed and frustrated.

HOW OTHERS FEEL

Being around a non-assertive person can leave others feeling frustrated. They might feel sorry for the person at first but then, having tried to help him/her and in some cases having received no response, they end up feeling irritated and annoyed.

CONSEQUENCES

Non-assertive people avoid taking responsibility and risks. They want to avoid rejection and the decision-making process. Many people who suffer from anxiety are often passive.

EXERCISE

Circle the words that best describe you.

Helpless	Powerless	Inadequate
Frustrated	Victim	Martyr
Over-committed	Poor confidence	Avoids responsibility
Not a risk-taker	Avoids rejection	Hard on self

Aggressive

PERSONAL FEELINGS

Aggressive people often feel out of control. Although they may feel superior in the short term, they may also feel fearful, insecure, and suffer from a lack of confidence.

SIGNS OF AGGRESSION

- You shout, bully, and use verbal and/or physical force to get your own way.
- You feel you must 'win' at all costs and anything except getting your own way is 'failure'.
- You do not respect the rights of other people.

HOW OTHERS FEEL

Someone exhibiting aggressive behaviour can make others feel scared, angry, helpless, and used.

CONSEQUENCES

Aggressive people tend to dominate. Their aggressive behaviour means they do not need to explain, negotiate, or listen to others. However, in the longer term, an aggressive person may become isolated and lose the respect of others.

EXERCISE

Circle the words that best describe you.

Shouts   Hits objects Bullies others Wags finger

Superior Fearful   Insecure   Poor confidence

Indirectly aggressive/passive–aggressive

PERSONAL FEELINGS

When you behave in a passive–aggressive manner you may feel frustrated, disappointed, and lacking in confidence.

SIGNS OF INDIRECTLY AGGRESSIVE/ PASSIVE–AGGRESSIVE BEHAVIOURS

- You are unpredictable. One day you agree and the next you disagree about the same subject.
- You hold grudges and bide your time to pay back others.
- You sulk and are able to generate a difficult atmosphere around you.

HOW OTHERS FEEL

A passive–aggressive person can make others feel angry, hurt, confused, manipulated, and guilty.

CONSEQUENCES

This type of behaviour is aimed at avoiding direct confrontation and rejection and often leads to a breakdown in relationships.

EXERCISE

Circle the words that best describe you.

Frustrated   Disappointed   Lacking in confidence

Holds grudges Uses 'pay-back' Sulks

Avoids confrontation

Assertive

PERSONAL FEELINGS

An assertive person often feels relaxed and confident. Assertiveness does not provide immunity against experiencing difficult emotions and an assertive person has a full range of emotions. However, an assertive person can choose the appropriate behaviour to use.

SIGNS OF ASSERTIVENESS

- I ask for what I want.
- I attempt to be clear in what I say.
- I listen to the needs of others.
- I respect myself and other people.
- I aim for 'win-win' situations and am happy to compromise without seeing compromising as something negative.

HOW OTHERS REACT

An assertive person usually creates feelings in others of being valued, respected, and listened to. An assertive person's behaviour makes people feel safe, secure, and fairly treated.

CONSEQUENCES

Assertive people seize opportunities, develop healthy relationships, and feel genuinely confident.

Exercise

Circle the words that best describe you.

Confident   Relaxed   Listens to others

Win–win   Seizes opportunities   Respects others

Respects self

What assertiveness involves

Respect for self and for others

Assertive people respect themselves and other people equally. They choose to show this respect in the way they openly, honestly, and genuinely deal with other people. They will stand up for themselves. Setting boundaries is one way in which we show respect for ourselves. It is up to each individual to decide what boundaries to create.

For example – '*I appreciate that you do not have the authority to provide a refund, however, I would like to talk to someone who does have the authority*'.

Taking personal responsibility for thoughts, feelings, and actions

Assertive people are prepared to take responsibility for what they say, for what they feel, and for what they do. They realize how important it is to act in a responsible way.

For example, '*I feel put down when you shout at me*', is more assertive than '*You make me angry when you shout at me*'. Using the word 'I' is one way of taking responsibility for what you feel, think, say, and do – for example, '*I feel let down by this decision*'.

Recognizing and making choices

Assertive people recognize the need to make choices and do not avoid doing so. They believe that even if they make the wrong choice, it is not the end of the world. Assertiveness means taking risks and assertive people believe that life is based on acceptable risk-taking.

Some assertiveness skills

The three steps to assertiveness

STEP ONE

Listen to what the other person is saying and demonstrate that you have *heard* and *understood* what has been said. You are more likely to get the outcome you seek if the other person feels you have really heard him/her. Very often we are more concerned with what we want to say than what the other person has said, and this can lead to the pantomime situation of '*oh yes, you did*'; '*oh no, I didn't*'.

Will: '*I felt undermined by the way you cut in on me when we were speaking to that new client.*'

John: '*I can see how you might have felt that.*'

STEP TWO

In step two you say what you *think* or *feel*. If this stage is to flow smoothly, you need to use a *link* word or phrase such as 'however', or 'on the other hand', or 'alternatively'.

John: '*However, I did have some information you did not and I realized that we could end up making certain*

> *commitments we might not be able to fulfil, given the impact of this new information.'*

STEP THREE

In step three you say what you *want to happen*. To help this section flow from the one before you need to use the link word *and*. In step three you are looking for what could be called a workable compromise, something that will sort the situation out and help both parties learn something useful for the next time such a situation arises.

John: *'. . . and perhaps we could work out how we manage this kind of situation for next time.'*

Example

Step one:	*'I understand you want me to see you over Christmas . . .*
Link word:	*. . . however,*
Step two:	*I have my sister to consider as she is coming over from Australia*
Link word:	*and*
Step three:	*I need to talk to her first before I can give you an answer.'*

Managing instant reactions

Change takes time. If you find yourself reacting quickly count to three in your head and take a deep breath. This should slow you down so that you can make a more considered response.

Less is more

You may find you over-explain yourself in the answers you give. If this is the case try to keep what you say short and simple. After all, you can have more than one bite of the apple and do not have to say everything in one go.

More assertiveness skills

Broken record

There will be times when you have used the three-step model and the person seems to ignore what you say. In this case, you need to repeat what you have said in a consistent way until your message cannot be ignored. The idea is to restate the essence of what you are saying rather than always using the same words.

Example

Joe: '*I appreciate that you want me to decide on our holiday plans.*'

James: '*It's not that big a deal. Surely you can say yes or no now?*'

Joe: '*I can understand that it is frustrating for you. However, I do need to think about things and then come back to you, as my work has a number of projects on and I am not sure about the timing of these.*'

Negative feelings assertion

You need to identify the behaviour that troubles you, explain how it affects you, and say what you want to happen. For example, if someone is shouting at you, you may find it hard to listen to what is being said and you can say so. If the person is sulking, you may feel that you cannot get through to him/her to sort out what is wrong and this damages your feelings towards that person.

Example

'*I feel frustrated when you interrupt me* (the behaviour) *and find it really hard to keep my thoughts in order* (how it affects you) *and I do want to be able to give you a considered answer* (what you want to happen)'.

Workable compromise

This works on the basis of finding a solution that both of you can live with. It's about aiming for a 'win-win' situation. It means both of you compromising to come up with a solution you can both live with. People who aim to communicate in this way increase their bank of goodwill, as they see goodwill as a kind of investment that can be called upon later.

Example:

Sean: '*I really need you to help me sort my car out.*'
Roger: '*I'm really happy to help you. However, I am a bit busy at the moment and will ring you later today to fix a time.*'
Sean: '*I guess that's fair.*'

Deflecting

Deflecting can be used to diffuse aggressive situations. It is based on the principle that no one is perfect and only requires you to agree that the person making the statement has a right to his or her own point of view. If you agree with the person you are not selling out – just acknowledging their right to their own view. Most people are waiting for us to disagree with them, and all this disagreement gains is a game of '*oh yes you did – oh no I didn't*'. If you agree with part of what is being said, you can stop the situation from escalating.

Example

Mary: '*You always seem to know best and never credit me with having anything worthwhile to say.*' (This sort of statement could easily lead to a row.)

Delia: '*You may have a point. It wouldn't be my intention to come across like that but I guess it's possible that I do.*' (By agreeing only to the possibility, you act in a way which is non-defensive and defuses a potentially explosive situation.)

Discrepancy assertion

This skill simply requires you to highlight any inconsistencies in what is being said.

Example

'*On the one hand you say I never give you work that is challenging, and on the other you say that you find some of the work beyond you.*'

Thinking it over time

Changing behaviour takes time. If you have been someone who says 'yes' without thinking, you may find yourself continuing to do so. One way of breaking the cycle is to ask for thinking it over time. When asked something, take time to consider your position. If you are on the telephone, suggest that you ring the person back at a certain time – '*I can't speak now so let me ring you back in twenty minutes*'. If you are actually with someone, you can say, '*I need time to think about what you have said*'.

A quick trip to the loo is an effective way to buy time. A quick '*excuse me*', followed by a few minutes taking time to think about what you want to say, can provide the space you need to make a sensible decision.

My personal rights

> ## EXERCISE
>
> Consider the following statements and mark each box with 'A' or 'D' depending on whether you agree or disagree with them.
>
> - I have the right to be treated with respect as an equal human being. ☐
> - I have the right to ask for what I want. ☐
> - I have the right to look after my needs and say 'No'. ☐
> - I have the right to express my feelings and thoughts. ☐
> - I have the right to ask for time before making a decision. ☐
> - I have the right to make my own decisions. ☐
> - I have the right to change my mind. ☐
> - I have the right to refuse responsibility for other people's problems if I so choose. ☐
> - I have the right to choose not to be assertive. ☐

These rights are a way to get you thinking about how you value yourself. Alongside rights are also the responsibilities we have towards others. Assertiveness means respecting self and others equally. You do not have the right to infringe the rights of others and you give yourself the same rights you give other people.

> ## EXERCISE
>
> *What other rights do you want to add to those above?*

Dealing with difficult situations

Coping with conflict

No one gets through life without having to face conflict situations. Most people dislike conflict but many of us make the situation worse by the way we deal with it. Anxious people often avoid conflict and then feel put upon or not valued.

Assertiveness skills provide you with a set of skills to deal with what is said so that you can verbally influence a positive outcome.

Work towards a win/win outcome

Try to think about what you want and what you think the other person might want. See if you can give the other person something of what they want as this is more likely to make them amenable and get you more of what you want with the least hassle.

Separate yourself and the other person from the issue

When the temperature rises and when you want something, emotions such as anxiety can get in the way. Strong emotions block the ability to listen and think – both of which are required if conflict is to be resolved without damaging the relationship.

Take responsibility and make clear 'I' statements

You are responsible for your own thoughts and actions. If you want to handle conflict assertively you need to ensure you make clear 'I' statements as a way of demonstrating your needs and wants.

One issue at a time and know what you want to happen

Your conflict with a person may be about one issue or it may be about many issues. You might find you have bottled things up and that there is a danger of too many subjects being talked about at the same time. Successful conflict resolution means dealing with one subject at a time. This means making a list of all the things you want to talk about and then deciding which one to discuss first.

Give your undivided attention

You are far more likely to get a positive outcome if you can demonstrate your respect for the other person by the way you deal with them.

The right time and the right place

If you really want to resolve a situation, then think about when and where you are going to deal with it. There is also little point trying to resolve conflict if you are likely to be disturbed or in a crowded place. Choose a private location and time when both of you are free.

Dealing with requests

There are times when people will ask you to do something for them. If you are happy to say yes, then fine. However, many people say yes when they really want to say no. There are three options for dealing with requests, but before you can exercise one of these, you need to examine your feelings about the request.

IDENTIFYING WHAT YOU FEEL

Many people override their basic 'gut' reaction to a request, and some people not only override it, they don't even notice it. When someone makes a request, you may find yourself feeling uncomfortable in some way. If this is the case, ask yourself what you feel uncomfortable about. It may also help if you ask yourself the following questions.

> *Do I feel used in some way?*
> *Do I feel 'I have to' and, if so, why?*
> *What's the worst that could happen if I say no?*
> *What feeling am I experiencing* (anger, fear, embarrassment etc.)?

Once you are sure of your feelings, you can respond to the request using one of the following options.

OPTION ONE: SAYING 'NO'

If you want to say 'no', say so clearly. It is perfectly reasonable to provide an explanation, but don't excuse or justify yourself. If you over-explain it usually means you feel bad about saying no and are trying to justify your position.

OPTION TWO: SAYING 'YES'

If you want to say 'yes', say so clearly. If you are happy to say yes but want to modify what you are prepared to offer, then outline the conditions that apply.

OPTION THREE: NOT SURE

If you are not sure what you want:

- Ask for more information to help you make your decision.
- Ask for more time to consider your decision.

141

- Suggest a compromise if you believe this is appropriate.
- Watch out for an 'indirect no' – a way of trying to avoid saying no by stating things in ways that are aimed at getting the other person to take back the request.

Handling criticism

Many people believe that criticism means they are inadequate in some way or are being unfairly targeted as mentioned earlier.

You can handle criticism in the following ways.

- Be clear about what the criticism is about. Ask for more information.
- Ask for more time to consider what has been said. After all, it can be difficult to identify what you think or feel immediately.
- Ask for more information, if required, and then state clearly your need for time to consider what has been said. Wherever possible, tell the person when you will come back to him/her.
- Once you have thought about what has been said, you need to decide whether you think the criticism is valid or not. If you agree with what has been said, you need to accept the criticism and discuss any future changes. If you disagree with what has been said. then ensure you disagree confidently, making sure you do not apologize.

Giving criticism

Giving criticism can be as hard for some people as receiving it, especially for people who suffer from anxiety.

Holding on to negative feelings doesn't help. If you are a manager, you will have to give criticism to your staff at some time or another. If you are a parent, you will have to criticize your children from time to time, otherwise they may never learn and could go on to develop unhelpful ways of relating to others.

You can give criticism effectively using the following methods.

- Find a private place to have the discussion. If you want someone to think about what you are saying you need to respect his or her feelings.
- Find something good to say about the person's behaviour. Acknowledge the person's good points as well as bad points. Be genuine in what you say.
- Try to avoid becoming too personal. Keep your comments to the facts of the situation and how you feel.
- Criticize the person's behaviour. Behaviour is something people have control over, whereas there may be things about themselves that they cannot change; for example, whether they speak with an accent.
- Describe your feelings and how you are affected by the person's behaviour.
- Make sure you listen to what the other person has to say. Effective communication requires active participation and active listening.
- The other person needs to understand the consequence of not changing. If someone knows that a particular behaviour upsets you or damages your relationship, this can be enough to motivate him or her to change.

Managing put-downs

There are a number of different ways in which people may try to put you down, some of which are listed below.

1. *Making decisions for you*
   Trying to make a decision for you puts you down as it takes away your personal responsibility. If this is the case, you need to let the person know you are capable of making your own decisions. For example, '*I appreciate that you have my best interests at heart. However, I need to do this myself.*'

2. *Putting the pressure on you*
   Sometimes people drop something on us when we are least expecting it as a way of trying to force us to make a decision or go along with what they are saying. This type of action puts you on the spot. If this is the case you need to ask for time to think about what's being asked of you.

3. *Making claims that you are lying*
   A person may suggest directly or indirectly that what you have said is not true, the implication being that you are lying. If this is the case, you need to be clear about what you are saying. For example, '*It is my understanding that Jane was the last person to leave the office.*'

Using the 'traffic light' system

We have explored the concept of you recognizing your 'early warning systems' when it comes to experiencing anger – for example, learning that when you find yourself breathing faster, or fidgeting, or feeling hot, these physical reactions tell you that you are becoming angry. In addition, we have considered the way that you judge situations and the types of 'faulty thinking' you may engage in, and we have also considered the reality that change takes time.

One technique that some people have found helpful is that of using the imagery of a traffic light to help manage difficult situations.

Red   =   Stop
Amber =   Wait
Green =   Go

Red

When you are in a situation and feel your anger rising because this situation is either one of your triggers or because you recognize that you are getting angry, you visualize the red stop sign.

Amber

Now that you have stopped, you wait, and during this period you undertake whatever strategies you need to so that you gain the ability to control what you say and what you will do. For example, you may undertake the rescue remedy breathing exercise, identify your faulty thinking, and/or think about using the three-step model from the 'Assertiveness' section of this book. This is the stage where you wait, analyse, and plan what to do.

Green

Now that you have stopped (red), waited and plan-ned (amber) you can now take whatever action seems appropriate as you have the green light to go! By the time you get to green, you are more likely to act in a way that is helpful to you and to others.

The role of 'time out'

Although you may be very committed to changing your behaviour, you may not find it easy to overcome the angry habits that you have fallen into. Sometimes it is best to walk away from a situation to give yourself time to calm down. If you get angry with your partner when certain types of discussions come up, then it might be helpful if you agree with him or her that if you recognize that you are likely to get out of control you will engage in a strategy called 'time out'. Time out means walking away to another room, engaging in another activity until you can think clearly, or even going for a walk to cool down.

Time out is a short-term strategy, and one which is really useful as a fall-back position for those situations where it all gets out of hand and you fear you may act in a self-defeating manner.

The more you practise the other techniques in this book, the less you will need to use time out.

Learning how to argue

While some people avoid arguing by becoming ultra passive and refusing to say what they feel, others think that arguments provide an opportunity to insult the other person – often believing the only way to argue is to make sure you scream the loudest. There are also those that fall into a massive sulk the minute you disagree with whatever they say or do. All these behaviours harm a relationship – they make you feel bad about yourself and usually end up with both of you feeling hurt and rejected and you never really sort out the cause of the original disagreement.

Arguments are a part of life. You are not going to get to your deathbed without having an argument with someone, somewhere, at some time. The good news is – there is such a thing as a healthy argument. Healthy arguing takes practice and can be learned like any skill, and once you've cracked how to do it you'll find your disagreements far more productive.

If you want to strengthen your relationship you need to learn how to disagree. Healthy arguing means you get to know each other better – after all how can you know what someone is like if you never find out what they think? Learning how to argue will help you communicate more clearly and you'll end up feeling more respect for yourself and for others.

If you want to argue more successfully with family, friends, partners, your boss, and your work colleagues, then the following tips will help you.

Listen!

Start by listening to what the other person has to say and make sure you acknowledge their point of view. You don't have to agree with what they are saying, but you do need to show you've got the message. For example, *'From your point of view, I can see you might feel let down'*, or *'I get the feeling you think I'm not being supportive'*, or *'I know this is a full-on time for our department and you've a lot to think about'*. If you don't actively show that you have listened, the other person will assume that you haven't and will either walk away or withdraw because they will think you're not taking them seriously. Alternatively, they may increase the intensity of their argument and the volume of their voice in an attempt to make you listen.

Think about what's being said

It's all right to ask for time to think about what's being said – you don't have to answer instantly and you can come back to the discussion later. Make sure you tell the other person you need time to think, otherwise you could end up looking as if you're the one avoiding the issue rather than simply needing some space and time to think about it! Make the point that you respect what they have to say and therefore you believe they deserve a proper answer and not a half-baked one.

So you're always right then?

Does the other person have a point? If you think they do, agree, if not, state your reasons for disagreeing in as calm a way as possible. You may need more information before you can decide whether they do have a point or not, and if this is the case don't be afraid to ask for it. After all, how you can you decide one way or the other if you don't know what the other person is really talking about?

Stick to the point

Don't get side-tracked into other issues. Take one thing at a time. Make a list if you have to but keep to the point. Think about what you are trying to get out of the argument – for example, if you want to make a point, do so clearly and keep on repeating it as long as it takes to get the point home. Remember this is not about getting the other person to agree with you (although that would be nice), but simply about them hearing your point of view.

Don't try to talk about too many things at once. Very often when an argument starts it is tempting to bring up all sorts of events that you feel the other person did not handle well. However, all this does is prolong the argument and ends up like scoring points . . . 'and another thing . . .!'

Don't put off discussions for too long

If you put off having a discussion for too long it may mean that both of you have time for your feelings to fester. When you do this, what usually happens is you end up arguing about something else that is totally unrelated! Don't put your head in the sand. So many arguments could be avoided if people shared all the little things that bug them when they happen. People often tell me they don't want to say anything because it might sound petty. However, it's all those petty things that get stored up that one day get let out all at once, usually in a major argument over nothing at all.

Don't blame others

You are responsible for your *own feelings* – it is too easy to blame others. People are *not mind readers* – just because you think something doesn't mean the other person has to, or that you are right. People are brought up differently, with different rules about how to behave, and if you assume that all people should think the way you do, it will only lead to problems.

149

Can you remember the first time you went to a friend's house and saw his or her family doing something differently to your own? I imagine you thought it was odd, and up until that point you had thought everyone did everything the way your family did.

Look for a 'win-win'

Many people approach arguments as if they are a life and death situation. Research has shown that successful and happy people look for a 'win-win' in their disagreements with others. Compromise is not a dirty word – those who know how to compromise usually end up far better off than those who don't. What's the point of hurting your relationship just to prove you were right?

Learning the importance of listening

The ability to handle difficult situations and hold a conversation depends on being able to develop active listening skills. Good listening skills help you get to know the person you are speaking to and are also crucial in deepening relationships and helping sort out problems.

You need to *learn* how to:

LISTEN: to what the other person is saying and feedback the essence of what they are saying. Hold on to what you have to say till the other person has completed what he or she has to say.

EVALUATE/EMPATHIZE: remember what has been said and see if you can make connections. For example: '*You said earlier that you thought I had behaved badly, and you have been avoiding me recently, and I wonder if that is the reason?*' Does it sound as if the person is happy, sad, enthusiastic, or indifferent? Try to use these feelings in your conversation. For example: '*You sound quite put out!*' Empathy is the ability to put yourself in the other person's shoes. When someone talks to you, try to imagine how you would feel if you saw the world the way that person does.

And

RESPOND: a good listener is involved in the conversation and can sometimes anticipate what the speaker is going to say next. Don't complete people's sentences, but try to imagine where you think the conversation is going. Don't be frightened to add information of your own. For example: '*I know what you mean about how I can sound a bit overbearing. I find it hard when other people do that to me.*' To learn to become proficient at active listening takes time and practice. Active listening means developing your memory and concentration skills and these do get better in time. Try using these skills in as many places and with as many people as possible.

Now: although it is helpful to plan for difficult conversations it is also important to deal with situations as soon as you can. If you put things off then feelings can fester.

WHAT AN ANGER-FREE LIFE REQUIRES

You have the skills to improve the way you interact with other people, influencing a more positive outcome for yourself, although there are still some common areas of concern that you need to consider before you can really say you live an appropriately anger-free life.

Time management

If you are unable to manage your time effectively, you will not follow through on the promises you make yourself to improve your life. You might find yourself wanting and wishing things to be different, but saying you don't have enough time to practise your new skills.

Time is a valuable commodity. How many times do you catch yourself saying, '*I'd want to but don't have the time*', or '*There really does seem too much to do*'? Too much activity leads to exhaustion; too little and you could become bored and frustrated. There are 168 hours in a week and 8,736 hours in a 365-day year, and so, with a finite amount of time, it is important that you make the most of what you have.

EXERCISE

To help you consider your time management needs, think about the activities you are involved in on a weekly basis and list these in a copy of the table below.

ITEM	TIME ALLOCATION
e.g. Family commitments	
Travel	

How effectively do you allocate your time?

ASK YOURSELF THE FOLLOWING QUESTIONS:

1. Do I have time to do what I would like to?   Yes   No
2. Do I put off activities because I have too much to do?   Yes   No

153

3. Do I feel there simply is not enough time?   Yes   No
4. Have I ever thought about the way I use   Yes   No
   my time?
5. Am I happy about the way I allocate
   my time?   Yes   No

If you have answered yes to 2 and 3 and no to 1, 4, and 5, you might need to consider how you allocate your time and whether this is effective for you

Time can be divided into six areas and it may be helpful to draw a circle, labelling this your 'Time allocation pie' (Figure 9). Consider each of the six areas below and divide your pie into the portions that you believe accurately represents your allocation of time over a one-week period.

Work time	Time earmarked for work, paid or voluntary.
Home time	Time for housework/maintenance, personal care, and gardening.
'Other' time	Time for family, friends, and children.
'Me' time	Time for hobbies, relaxation, exercise, and sleep.
'Us' time	Time to spend with our partner.
Quiet time	Time to ourselves for thinking, evaluating, and reflecting (e.g., *how well you are doing at your learning to be your own life coach*).

If you are not happy with the amount of time you have allocated to any activity, consider how to reallocate the time you have so that you achieve the balance you are seeking. If there are slices of your pie that are greatly out

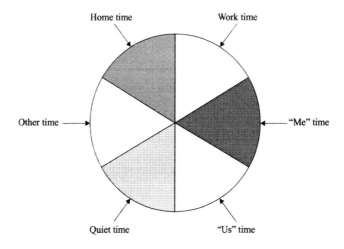

Figure 9. Time allocation pie

of balance, you may find it helpful to keep a written record of your feelings about how you have allocated your time over a one-week period.

Apart from completing the time allocation pie you could also consider:

1. How you manage your time.
2. How you fritter your time away.
3. How you could be more effective in managing your time.
4. How you could make more time to do the things you like.
5. How you could do less of the things you dislike.

At the end of a week you should have a better idea of how you spend your time and what you would like to create more or less time to do.

Your biological clock has an effect on time management as there are times of the day when you will feel more alert than others. For example, some people prefer mornings when they feel full of energy but find they feel exhausted mid-afternoon. If this is the case, it makes sense to try, wherever possible, to save your difficult tasks for the time of the day when you have most energy. Your best time of day is often called your 'prime time'.

Consider other people's 'prime time', as there may be times of the day when it would be better to approach certain people. If there are times of the day when you are more energetic why not seek out such times in others as this may help influence a positive outcome.

There are three aspects of time management to consider:

- checklists and notes as ways of keeping track of the work you have to do;
- calendars and appointment books for planning ahead;
- short-, medium-, and long-term goal setting and the recognition of your personal values and desires.

Poor organization

Poor organization can mean:

- poorly maintained filing system (e.g., *filing not done on a regular basis*) and valuable time lost looking for information;
- no system to identify relevant information (e.g. *papers and documentation simply thrown into a pile*);
- indiscriminately keeping everything that is received, filling valuable space as well as using time to locate items – the 'just in case' principle.

If you find yourself spending time on non-productive discussions either at work or with friends when you need to be doing something else, consider the following:

- keep conversations short;
- keep a clock nearby to remind you to deal with the call effectively;
- learn how to use the three-step model of assertiveness:

> Step one: I understand your problem, e.g., '*I do appreciate you need to meet with me*'.
> Step two: However, I think or feel, e.g., '*However, I need to do some research*',
> Step three: and I suggest, e.g., '*and I suggest we speak at the end of the week when I have all the information*

Diaries, personal and electronic organizers

A diary, a personal or an electronic organizer, are mechanisms to keep track of appointments and are good for planning ahead. If you use a diary or personal organizer you may also find it useful to mark your appointments in pencil, as this allows them to be changed with the minimum of fuss. If you choose to use an electronic organizer, you need to back up your data on a regular basis to protect against loss of information.

To do lists

A '*to do*' list is a form of memory aid. In addition to recording tasks to be done, a simple system such as A, B and C can be used as a way of organizing priorities.

A = Urgent items which require immediate attention.
B = Important items which require attention in the near future.
C = Non-essential or non-urgent items.

Post-it notes

Some people find it helpful to place post-it notes in full view to remind them to carry out urgent tasks.

Filing systems

A portable, lockable, metal filing system can prove useful to help you store household documentation. Being able to find something first time can really save you time.

Effective time management means thinking about what you do, how you do it, and how you can make the most of this finite resource. Unlike most items, time cannot be stored for future use.

To ensure that you use your time effectively, you need to build in 'quiet' time as a legitimate activity. This type of activity enables you to evaluate the present while considering the future.

Stress busting

As you saw earlier, stress involves a complex relationship between the demands made of a person and the personal and external resources he or she has to meet these demands. These demands can trigger the stress response (see p. 5).

The demands that are made of you could be 'internal'; that is, your own thinking style. Perfectionists put pressure on themselves and this is therefore an internal demand, as no one else is making it. Resources comprise factors such as your physical health, financial security, social and family support. Keep a balance so that you do not have more demands than resources to deal with them.

If demands exceed your resources you may feel you cannot cope, and this is the beginning of what has become known as stress.

Some people talk about healthy and unhealthy stress, meaning that some stress is good for you. It is easier to think in terms of the idea of 'pressure' and 'stress'. Pressure is healthy, and something that can motivate you. Some people love to live in a pressured way, with lots of deadlines and things to do. The distinction between pressure and stress is that you experience pressure when you have the resources you need to deal with the demands being made of you. Pressure turns to stress when the pressure becomes too great, lasts too long, comes suddenly, and ends up with you feeling it cannot be controlled.

Stress is a very personal matter. A situation that might stress your friend may not affect you, and vice versa. An event may have proved stressful to you at one point in our life, but you may have developed additional resources to deal with the situation as you have grown older.

Work can be a great source of stress: time pressures, excessive workload, poor relations with colleagues/ managers, poor communications within your organization, being exposed to continual change, not being trained to do the job, and job insecurity all play their part. Stress can be experienced in your personal life: family problems, life changes/crises, increasing demands between home and work – all may affect you.

In 1967, Thomas Holmes and Richard Rahe, two American psychologists, first published a scale of forty-three life events considered to be stressful. Each event was scored according to the degree of stress associated with it. Listed below are the top seven items, together with the score associated with each event.

The life event	Score
Death of a partner	100
Divorce	73
Marital separation	65
Imprisonment	63
Death of a close family member	63
Personal illness or injury	53
Marriage	50

In addition to the above, other items included:

- dealing with Christmas;
- pregnancy;
- sexual difficulties;
- legal action;
- moving house;
- changing school or college;
- change in living conditions;
- change in hours or working conditions;
- arguments with partners or family;
- adoption or birth of a child.

One of the advantages of understanding the impact of life events is that it can help you anticipate stressful events. For example, knowing that having a baby can be stressful allows you to consider what stress management techniques are likely to help you. A fact that surprised many people was that life events seen as pleasurable also carried a stress rating; for example, getting married, having a baby, or gaining a promotion. Good experiences usually entail a degree of change, and it can be the changes to lifestyle and the need to develop new coping skills that contribute to the stress experienced.

THE ANGER-FREE DIET

Anger and dietary tips

Anger can be made worse by taking stimulants such as tea, coffee, colas, and chocolate, all of which contain caffeine. Caffeine is a stimulant, and stimulants are best avoided when we are experiencing emotions such as anger. Because we produce stress hormones when we are feeling angry, this can affect our blood sugar levels, and they may indeed drop dramatically. Therefore, in order to keep those levels balanced, it is important to eat 'little and often' during the day. It may also be helpful to avoid refined sugars and other substances that 'give too much of a high' too quickly. Slow-release foods such as carbohydrates (potatoes, pasta, rice, bread, apples, and bananas) are a much better idea as they fuel the body in a more even, controlled way.

These days it is impossible to avoid information on healthy eating. However, what we eat also has an effect on our confidence levels and our ability to cope emotionally.

As was outlined in the 'Stress busting' section above, our bodies produce stress hormones and release fatty acids and sugars to help us cope with a perceived crisis. When such events take place our bodies' natural blood sugar levels are disturbed, and this is also the case when we become angry or anxious. Our blood sugars help us regulate the fuel requirements needed by our bodies. Low blood sugar or hypoglycaemia contributes to symptoms of anxiety.

A drop in blood sugar causes reactions in the nervous system, including feelings of anxiety (which can fuel anger). Diets that contain large amounts of refined sugars, or are deficient in protein or fat, together with the use of stimulants such as coffee or cola based drinks, contribute to this condition.

You may be lacking in magnesium, zinc, and the amino acid tryptophan. Alternatively, an excessive amount of some nutrients can speed up your nervous system and this can provide the breeding ground for anger. Potassium, sodium, phosphorus, and copper are just such minerals.

If the thyroid or adrenal glands become overactive, such conditions affect the way we feel, as we cannot absorb and use sufficient minerals and, as a result, anxiety may follow. An underactive thyroid is more likely to lead to feelings of depression than of anxiety.

What can I do to help myself?

If you have any concerns at all about your health, your first port of call should be your doctor. I have always believed that all medical conditions should be eliminated before considering any emotional and/or life factors.

We are all aware that eating a healthy diet is good for our overall health. However, there is research that suggests that eating certain types of food can have a positive effect on the way in which we behave. For example, you will see that under 'What foods can I eat?' I have listed fish/shellfish under protein. The reason for this is that omega-3 DHA (an essential fatty acid) has been linked with helping control behavioural conditions such as depression, alcoholism, and aggressive behaviour.

The following are some dietary tips that will help you.

- Drink plenty of water – not only is it good for your skin, it helps flush out toxins and keeps your kidneys in good working order. Around eight large glasses a day is best. There is nothing wrong with flavouring the water if you are not keen on drinking water. However, avoid sugary flavourings as this will defeat the object. Drinking fruit teas are also a good way of getting water down you.
- Make sure you eat at least six times a day. Breakfast, mid-morning, lunch, mid-afternoon, tea, and dinner. By eating little and often and ensuring you do not skip meals you will help your blood sugar levels stay balanced.
- Keep healthy snacks around you and plan ahead for days when it may be difficult to find healthy meals.
- Try to avoid 'fast food', as it usually contains more fat and additives than are good for you.
- Take a multi-vitamin pill daily. It can be difficult to ensure you get all the nutrients you need through the food you eat and a multi-vitamin tablet will help ensure you are topped up on any you may be missing. A good option for people who don't like fish is to take Omega-3 DHA capsules. However, it is best if you can get your vitamins directly from the food you eat rather than simply from pills.
- Try to avoid coffee, tea, cola drinks, and chocolate, as all these contain varying amounts of caffeine. It would be a sad world if you could not allow yourself a little of what you fancy, so if you want chocolate now and again, buy the more expensive kind which has a higher concentration of cocoa solids and less sugar.

- Try to avoid saturated fats, as these can lead to health problems. A diet that is high in fat will also contain high levels of cholesterol. There is an increased risk of cancer of the breast, colon, and prostate, as well as coronary heart disease.
- Try to avoid an excess of alcohol – alcohol dehydrates, is a depressant, and can increase mood swings and depressive symptoms and fuel aggression. In addition, alcohol rather than aiding sleep actually impairs it and when you are tired you are likely to be more irritable. In addition, it can deplete vitamin B levels in the body, and vitamin B is linked with aiding a healthy nervous system.
- Avoid excessive amounts of salt (sodium) as about a quarter of what we require is to be found naturally present in food. We require so little that we can quite happily survive on what occurs in our daily food.

What food can I eat?

The aim is to eat as varied a diet as possible. However, the following categories provide you with a more detailed breakdown of a range of foods that contribute to good physical and psychological health.

Protein

- Meat, chicken
- Fish, shellfish (Omega-3 DHA is an essential fatty acid and the best source is oily fish such as salmon, mackerel, sardines, and tuna)
- Dried beans
- Soya products

Carbohydrates

COMPLEX

- Wholegrain bread
- Pasta
- Rice
- Peas and beans
- Vegetables
- Fruit and nuts

Refined sugar (not so helpful)

- Sweet foods.

Calcium

- Milk, cheese, yoghurt
- Fish
- Broccoli, spring greens, leeks, cabbage, parsnips, potatoes, blackberries, and oranges

Potassium

- Potatoes and sweet potatoes
- Fish, sardines
- Pork, chicken
- Cauliflower, sweetcorn, avocados, leeks
- Breakfast cereals,
- Natural yoghurt
- Bananas, rhubarb

Iron

- Eggs
- Lean meat
- Wholegrain cereals

- Peas, beans, spinach, leeks, broccoli, spring greens, potatoes, avocados
- Dried fruit

Zinc and copper

- Liver and kidney, chicken
- Oysters
- Soya flour, cocoa powder
- Rice, bulgar wheat
- Beans, parsnips, plantain
- Pears

WHAT TYPE OF HELP
IS AVAILABLE?

The Royal College of Psychiatrists has recommended a number of ways in which an individual can seek help.

Talking about the problem

This can help when the anger comes from recent knocks, like a spouse leaving, a child becoming ill, bereavement, or losing a job. Who should we talk to? Try friends or relatives whom you trust, whose opinions you respect, and who are good listeners. They may have had the same problem themselves, or know someone else who has. As well as having the chance to talk, we may be able to find out how other people have coped with a similar problem.

Self-help groups

These are a good way of getting in touch with people with similar problems. They will be able to understand what you are going through, and may also be able to suggest helpful ways of coping. These groups may be focused on anxieties and phobias, or may be made up of people who have been through similar experiences – women's groups, bereaved parents' groups, survivors of abuse groups.

Anger management groups

These are similar to self-help groups, except that they are often supervised by a therapist and are likely to be more like a training programme in nature, although there may also be scope for one-to-one meetings with a therapist as well as group activities and support.

Learning to relax

It can be a great help to learn a special way of relaxing, to help control anger and tension. Such techniques can be learnt through groups or through professionals, but there are also self-help books and videotapes (see below). It's a good idea to practise these regularly, not just when we are in a crisis situation.

Psychological therapies

This is a more intensive talking treatment that can help people to understand and to come to terms with reasons for their anger that they may not have recognized themselves. The treatment can take place in groups or individually, and is usually weekly for several weeks or months. Therapists may or may not be medically qualified.

If this is not enough, there are several different kinds of professionals who may be able to help – the family doctor, psychiatrist, psychologist, social worker, nurse, or counsellor.

USEFUL RESOURCES

Materials

Biodots

Biodots can be purchased by contacting:
Centre for Stress Management
Broadway House
3 High Street
Bromley, BR1 1LF
Tel: 020 8228 1185

Useful organizations

Alcohol Concern
Waterbridge House
32–36 Loman Street
London SE1 OEE
Tel: 0207 928 7377
Provides information on alcohol and its effects and can provide details of alcohol agencies, residential, advice, and drop-in, across the UK.

Alzheimer's Society
Gordon House
10 Greencoat Place
London SW1P 1PH
Tel: 020 7306 0606
Helpline: 0845 300 0336
www.alzheimers.org.uk
Information and support for carers; campaigns, research.

Association for Rational Emotive Behaviour Therapists
St George's
Winter Street
Sheffield S3 7ND
Tel: 0114 271 6926
www.rebt.bizland.com
Professional body for therapists using Rational Emotive
Behaviour Therapy that can provide details of therapists.

Brake (Trauma Advisory Services – TAS)
PO Box 272
Dorking
Surrey RH4 4FR
Tel: 01306 741113
www.brake.org.uk
Provides information, advice, and guidance for those
involved in trauma following road traffic accidents.

British Association for Counselling and Psychotherapy
1 Regent Place
Rugby
Warwickshire CV21 2PJ
Tel: 0788 578 328
www.counselling.co.uk
Professional body for counsellors and psychotherapists in
the UK who can provide lists of therapists as well as information and advice on counselling.

British Association for Behavioural and Cognitive Psycho-
therapies
PO Box 9
Accrington BB5 2GD
Tel: 01254 875277
www.babcp.com

Professional Body for Psychiatrists, Psychologists, Counsellors and all those who use cognitive–behavioural techniques. Can provide lists of therapists and also information on cognitive–behavioural psychotherapies.

British Psychological Society
St Andrew's House
48 Princess Road East
Leicester LE1 7DR.
Tel: 0116 254 9568
www.bps.org.uk
Professional body for psychologists that can also provide details of psychologists.

Carers National Association
20 Glasshouse Yard
London EC1A 4JS
Tel. 0207 490 8818
Carersline – advice line for carers at the cost of a local call: 0345 573 369
Association that provides help, advice and support to those who care for others.

Centre for Stress Management
Centre for Stress Management
Broadway House
3 High Street
Bromley, BR1 1LF
Tel: 020 8228 1185
www.managingstress.com
Provides information and advice on stress-related issues, together with counselling and psychotherapy. Also offers training in a variety of subjects, including stress and post trauma stress, to a range of professionals.

Child Bereavement Trust
Tel: 01628 488101
Dedicated information and support line 0845 357 1000
www.childbereavement.org.uk
Offers information, advice and support to anyone who has
experienced the death of a child and for bereaved children.

Child Traumatic Stress Clinic
Michael Rutter Centre for Children and Adolescents
Maudsley Hospital
Denmark Hill
LONDON
SE5 8AZ
Tel: 020 7919 2546
www.slam.nhs.uk
Offers counselling, advice and support to parents and to
children who have experienced traumatic events.

COSCA (Confederation of Scottish Counselling Agencies)
18 Viewfield Street
Stirling FK8 IUE
Tel: 01786 476140
www.cosca.org.uk
Professional body for counsellors in Scotland that can
provide details of counsellors and information on counselling and counselling services.

CRUSE Bereavement Care
Cruse House
126 Sheen Road
Richmond
Surrey TW9 1UR
Tel: 0208 940 4818
www.crusebereavementcare.org.uk

Offers information, advice and counselling to those who have been bereaved with local branch offices across the country.

Compassionate Friends
53 North Street
Bristol BS3 1EN
Tel: 0117 966 5202
Helpline: 08451 23 23 04
www.tcf.org.uk
Organization offering advice, counselling, and support to those who have been bereaved, with local branches across the country.

Divorce Conciliation and Advisory Service
38 Ebury Street
London SW1W OLU
Tel: 0207 730 2422
Provides information, advice, counselling, and support.

Drinkline (The National Alcohol Helpline)
Petersham House
57 Hatton Garden
London EC1N 8HP
Tel: 0345 320202
Offers advice, counselling, and support to all those with alcohol-related problems.

DrugScope
Waterbridge House
32 – 36 Loman Street
London SE1 0EE
Tel: 020 7928 1211
www.drugscope.org.uk

Provides information on drug misuse and details of services across the country.

Ex-Services Mental Welfare Society (also known as Combat Stress)
Tyewhitt House
Oaklawn Road
Leatherhead
Surrey KT22 OBX
Tel: 01372 841600
www.combatstress
Provides information, advice, counselling, and support.

Families Need Fathers
134 Curtain Road
London EC2A 3AR
Tel: 0207 613 5060
www.fnf.org.uk
Provides information, advice and support for men experiencing difficulties with child access or who are finding it difficult to come to terms with limited child access.

International Stress Management Association (UK)
Department of Psychology
South Bank University
103 Borough Road
London SE1 OAA.
www.isma.org.uk
Tel: 07000 780430
Provides information, advice and details of stress management practitioners and trainers.

MIND
Granta House
15–19 Broadway
Stratford
London E15 4BQ
Tel: 020 8519 2122
Mind Information Line 0845 766 0163
www.mind.org.uk
Advice and information service on mental health problems.

National Council for One Parent Families
255 Kentish Town Road
London NW5 2LX
Tel: 020 7428 5400
Helpline: 0800 018 5026 Calls are free and confidential.
www.oneparentfamilies.org.uk
Offers information, advice and support on a range of
issues affecting one parent families.

Relate
Herbert Gray College
Little Church Street
Rugby
Warwickshire CV21 3AP
Tel: 0870 601 2121
www.relate.org.uk
Provides counselling for couples.

Relaxation for Living
29 Burwood Park Road
Walton-on-Thames
Surrey KT12 5LH
Tel: 01932 227826
www.relaxationforliving.co.uk

Courses and information on how to deal with stress.

Release
388 Old Street
London EC1V 9LT
Tel: 020 7928 1211
Helpline: 020 7729–9904
www.release.org.uk
Provides advice and information on drug misuse.

SAD Association
PO Box 989
Steyning
West Sussex BN44 3HG
Tel: 01903 814942
Web: www.sada.org.uk
Information, newsletter, and support for seasonal affective disorder.

Samaritans
10 The Grove
Slough
Berkshire
Tel: 01753 532713 or 0345 90 90 90
www.befrienders.org
Telephone counselling and drop-in centres.

UKRC (United Kingdom Register of Counsellors)
1 Regent Place
Rugby
Warwickshire CV21 2PJ
Tel: 0870 443 5232
www.bacp.co.uk
Register of counsellors in the UK

UKCP (United Kingdom Council for Psychotherapy)
167 Great Portland Street
London W1N 5FB
Tel: 0207 436 3002
www.psychotherapy.org.uk
Register of psychotherapists in the UK

Victim Support
Cranmer House
39 Brixton Road
London SW9 1DZ
Tel: 0207 735 9166
www.victimsupport.com
Offers information, advice, counselling, and support to those who have been the victims of crime. Local branches.

Appendices

Faulty thinking form

Situation	Self defeating thinking	Feelings and actions	Healthy response	New approach
A	B	C	D	E

Mood form

Situation	Good mood	Bad mood
I think . . .	I think . . .	

Understanding what upsets me

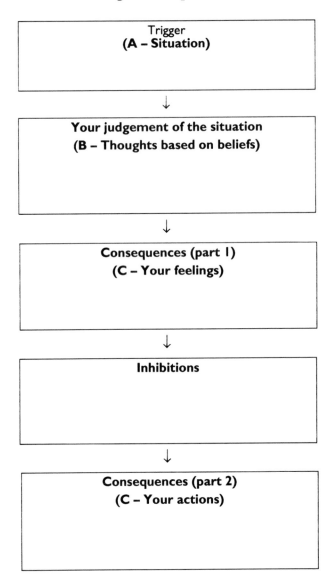

Trigger
(A – Situation)

↓

Your judgement of the situation
(B – Thoughts based on beliefs)

↓

Consequences (part 1)
(C – Your feelings)

↓

Inhibitions

↓

Consequences (part 2)
(C – Your actions)

Responsibility pie

Anger diary

Date	Time	Situation (trigger)	What I did

Cost–benefit analysis

Name: Date:

Situation:

COST	BENEFIT

Personal contingency plan

Feeling (rate 0–10)

What could go wrong?	What could I do if this happens?
1.	1.
2.	2.
3.	3.
4.	4.
5.	5.
6.	6.

Contact me

I am keen to know if my books are of help to readers and in what ways I can improve the information provided. If you would like to comment you can email me at gladeana@dircon.co.uk or you can send a letter to me via the publishers of this book.

INDEX